Date Due

BOOKS BY WAYNE ANDREWS

Architecture in Chicago and Mid-America   *1968*

Architecture in Michigan   *1967*

Germaine: A Portrait of Madame de Staël   *1963*

Architecture in America   *1960*

Best Short Stories of Edith Wharton (editor)   *1958*

Architecture, Ambition and Americans   *1955*

Who Has Been Tampering with These Pianos?   *1948*
   (under the pseudonym Montagu O'Reilly)

Battle for Chicago   *1946*

The Vanderbilt Legend   *1941*

ARCHITECTURE IN CHICAGO AND MID-AMERICA

ARCHITECTURE IN CHICAGO & MID-AMERICA

A PHOTOGRAPHIC HISTORY

WAYNE ANDREWS

NEW YORK ATHENEUM 1968

FOR MY FATHER, EMORY COBB ANDREWS

PHOTOGRAPHIC CREDITS AND ACKNOWLEDGMENTS

I am indebted to Richard Nickel, 1508 Grove Avenue, Park Ridge, Ill., for his photographs of the interior of the Schiller Building (49), the Wainwright Building (51) and the entrance to the Chicago Stock Exchange (53); to Leco Photo Service, 1 East 42nd Street, New York City, and to R. Buckminster Fuller for the photographs of the Climatron (176) and the exterior and interior of the Fuller house at Carbondale (177); to Hedrich Blessing, 450 East Ontario Street, Chicago, for the photograph of the lakefront reproduced in the introduction and for photographs of the Federal Center (168), the Farnsworth house (169) and the Inland Steel Building (170); to the Chicago Historical Society for the photographs of the exterior and interior of the Palmer House (21), the Marshall Field residence (22), the MacVeagh residence (24), the Administration Building (61), the Agricultural and the Manufactures Buildings (62), the Fisheries Building (63), and the Transportation Building (64); to the Chicago Architectural Photographing Co., 75 East Wacker Drive, Chicago, for photographs of the Marshall Field warehouse (23), the Potter Palmer castle (29), the Home Insurance Building (36), the Tacoma Building (38), the Monadnock Building (40), the Woman's Temple (41), the Masonic Temple (42), the Schiller Building (48), the exterior and interior of the Avery Coonley residence (78 and 79), the Midway Gardens (81) and the Chapin & Gore Building (86).

All other photographs are my own.

But I owe the greatest debt of all to Richard Schuler, Ernest Pile, Sybil Collins and the other members of the staff of Compo Photo Service, 220 West 42nd Street, New York, who have so carefully developed and enlarged my negatives and given me the benefit of their experience. This book would have been impossible without their complete co-operation.

The quotations from Louis Sullivan's *Autobiography of an Idea* are reproduced by courtesy of the American Institute of Architects.

Many architects have been helpful, especially Barry Byrne, the late George Grant Elmslie, the late Mrs. Walter Burley Griffin (Marion Mahony), the late William Gray Purcell, and Benjamin and Harry Weese. Aline Saarinen was so kind as to arrange a meeting with Eero Saarinen.

And many other people have been enlightening. Leonard K. Eaton discussed his forthcoming book on the clients of Wright and Shaw. W. Hawkins Ferry, author of the forthcoming *Buildings of Detroit* (Wayne University Press, 1968), answered innumerable questions about the architecture of Michigan. Mrs. Sidney Haskins helped me explore the work of her father, Howard Van Doren Shaw. Roger G. Kennedy gave me priceless advice on the subject of Harvey Ellis. Mrs. Paul M. Rhymner of the Chicago Historical Society saved me an immense amount of time while I was checking the Society's picture files. E. P. Richardson discovered for me the Allen house in Des Moines. Dimitri Tselos generously let me read his forthcoming article on the World's Fair of 1893 for the *Journal of the Society of Architectural Historians*, and Thomas C. Cochran was so obliging as to read the introduction.

Finally, Mr. and Mrs. Harwell Hamilton Harris have been more than enlightening.

v

INTRODUCTION:

Chicago has always meant all things to all men.

To Mrs. Astor's great and good friend Ward McAllister, America's second city was capable of infinite improvement. "The contact of New York and Chicago society cannot help but open the eyes of our Western natives to our superiority," he explained on the eve of the World's Fair of 1893. "I do not wish to belittle Chicago in using the word *superiority*. The society of Chicago is behind that of New York, but there is no reason why it should not eventually catch up. Chicago is moving in the right direction and should be encouraged in every way."

On the other hand, the packer Gustavus Franklin Swift thought Chicago was good enough as it was. Here, he implored a reporter to remember, "is the finest city in the world for the moderate, natural, average man of affairs in which to live. The New Yorker who says Chicago is a city of no luxuries is probably one of that constantly growing number who are insatiable in their greed for the softer things of life. To those men who have families and who find in their homes the greatest of their pleasures, Chicago offers all that New York offers, and in my opinion more. A man can get wholesome food in Chicago more cheaply than he can in the East, and he can live as well on a smaller amount of money. I do not go in for luxuries myself."

So much for the verdict of McAllister and Swift. To architects and to that apparently growing number of people who find architecture a fascinating subject, *Chicago is where it happened*. They know that Chicago can claim, as can no other city, to be the birthplace of modern architecture.

Ambition was in the air as early as 1883, when William Le Baron Jenney, an engineer lately on the staffs of Sherman and Grant, invented the eleven-story Home Insurance Building for the southwest corner of LaSalle and Adams Streets. This is gener-ally considered to be the world's first skyscraper: that is, the world's first tall steel-frame building. To be technical for a moment, wrought iron formed the skeleton up to and including the sixth story; beyond that point Bessemer steel beams were used. Whether or not the skeleton in this instance did *all* the work of the walls has been debated; there are those who insist that the honor of being the world's first must be assigned the Tacoma Building, conceived three years later for the northeast corner of LaSalle and Madison by the firm of Holabird & Roche. Whichever way you have it, Chicagoans were the first to prove that walls were no longer needed to perform the ancient function of support. Hereafter walls could be thin as silk, as Viollet-le-Duc had been arguing in France from his studies of the engineering of the Gothic cathedrals.

What began with the Home Insurance and Tacoma Buildings could not be arrested. Daniel Hudson Burnham and John Wellborn Root, greater artists by far than the gentlemen just mentioned, worked their sure will on tall buildings, and by 1889 the firm of Adler & Sullivan completed the incomparable Auditorium, a hotel combined with an opera house of unimpeachable acoustics. Out of the Adler & Sullivan office came Frank Lloyd Wright, who shattered in his twenties the useless conventions governing the design of the American home. "Democracy," cried Wright, "needed something basically better than the box." Chicago began setting the standards and Chicago architects began invading not only Saint Louis and the Twin Cities but the entire Middle West. This marvelous momentum came to a temporary halt in the 1920s, but Eliel Saarinen, who did his best to redeem the decade by his work at Cranbrook near Detroit, might never have left Finland for America if he had not won second prize in the contest for Chicago's Tribune Tower. And his son Eero Saarinen might never have arrived at the lethal accuracy of the General Motors Technical Center at Warren, Michigan—the most distinguished monument yet erected to the glory of a giant corporation—if he had not watched Ludwig Miës van der Rohe, the German who settled in Chicago in 1938, at work on the campus of the Illinois Institute of Technology. As for Albert Kahn, the Detroiter who became the master designer of factories, he too was Chicago-inspired when he laid out the General Motors Building in Detroit, which owes so much to the classical message of Burnham's last skyscrapers.

This is not the same thing as saying that Chicago either was or is paradise on earth. In the late nineteenth and early twentieth centuries it was a haunted city, as romantic or impractical in its way as the Old South. From which you must not infer that wisteria takes kindly to the soil of Illinois. Chicago lived in the shadow of its great millionaires, whose pronouncements on every subject were accorded the reverence the South granted the dying words of Stonewall Jackson.

Now that the millionaires have been brought back to mind, this may be the moment to listen to the singular complaint of the Chicago novelist Henry B. Fuller. "This town of ours," he decided back in 1895, "labors under one peculiar disadvantage: it is the only great city in the world to which all of its citizens have come for the one common, avowed object of making money. There you have its genesis, its growth, its end and object; and there are very few of us who are not attending to that object very strictly. In this Garden City of ours every man cultivates his own little bed and his neighbor his; but who looks after the paths between?"

Fuller did not need to be told that leisure in Chicago was usually regarded as an invitation to sin. Erastus Brainerd, the banker in his novel *The Cliff-Dwellers*, "had never lived for anything but business. . . . He never dreamed of anything but business—he had never worn a dress-coat in his life. He wrote about nothing but business—his nearest relative was never more than 'dear sir' and he himself was never more than 'yours truly'; and he wrote on business letterheads even to his own family.".

In Chicago life was earnest, no doubt of that. Wit and grace could not be easily commanded. It is true that Julia Loomis Newberry, whose father's fortune built the Newberry Library, might have brought the touch of Jane Austen to bear on the North Side, but she did not live to write the novels for which she was so exquisitely prepared. When barely twenty-two she died of tuberculosis in Rome, leaving merely her diary, in which at fifteen she proclaimed that her father's New York friend Stuyvesant Fish "in spite of his having a grandfather" was "little less than an idiot."

Wit and grace may be ingredients without which no literary or artistic center can exist, but architects, as the history of Chicago triumphantly proves, can not only survive but thrive in a serious-minded environment. The strange charm of Chicago, recalling in an oblique way that of the South, may be said to reside in the conflict between the strenuous ideals of the great businessmen and the demands of everyday life. The South could not live, and it has not lived, on the capital bequeathed by Robert E. Lee: a superb manner is not necessarily an asset in running a grocery store. Nor could Chicago *quite* conform to the commandments of Swift, Armour and Field: the very attempt would have been inhuman.

Except for Cyrus Hall McCormick, a sturdy Scotch-Irish immigrant from the Back Parts of Virginia, the great Chicago millionaires seem to have come from small towns in New England or from those regions of New York State overrun by New Englanders. The East they remembered was not Boston or Concord but some hamlet where the reading of Ralph Waldo Emerson was confined to the quarters of an eccentric schoolmaster.

Philip Danforth Armour, a native of Stockbridge, Madison County, New York, might be considered typical, if that be any way to describe the businessman who came closer than anyone else to being the folk hero of the city. "My culture is mostly in my wife's name," he confided to Elbert Hubbard, who did not hesitate to report that the packer's vocabulary "needed to be put on a buffing wheel. His stories often required formaldehyde."

"You have made your pile; why not clear out?" Armour was one day asked by a reporter. "I have no other interest in life but my business," came the answer. "I do not want any more money; as you say, I have more than I want. I do not love the money. What I do love is the getting of it. All these years of my life I have put into this work, and now it is my life and I cannot give it up. What other interest can you suggest to me? I do not read. I do not take any part in politics. What can I do? Besides, I think it is well for me to remain in business to set an example to the younger men who are coming up around me."

He did set an example. He liked to get down to work "before the boys with the polished nails show up," which meant that he got to the office at seven. He stayed there until six in the evening, occasionally staring stubbornly at the bunch of fresh flowers his secretary stuck in the ox-horn vase on his desk. At nine o'clock, having had a wholesome dinner in his own home on Prairie Avenue, he went straight to bed. There was nothing eccentric about his habits, and policemen were accustomed to set their watches by his coming and going.

"When I am done with work," he told a favorite employee, "remember this—that I always had a great respect for facts. If there were fewer theorists in the world, there would be more successes. Facts can be discounted in any bank, but a theory is rarely worth par. Stick to facts." He had grown up near the socialist community of Oneida but had never been tempted by the ideology of John Humphrey Noyes. "Oneida is for those whose dream did not come true," he chortled. "Mine has."

But there was one unpleasant fact that Armour was obliged to face, and that was the presence, nearby on Prairie Avenue, of Marshall Field. The master of the great department store did not leave home until nine in the morning, and invariably closed his desk at four in the afternoon. "I have never believed in overworking, either as applied to myself or others," he made plain. "It is paid for with a short life, and I do not believe in it."

The hours that Field kept were a constant mortification to Armour. "It must be wonderful to have a business like yours . . . and keep banker's hours," the packer rebuked the merchant prince when they were aboard a private car on an inspection trip of the Chicago, St. Paul & Milwaukee Railroad. On this very trip Field made the mistake of proposing a game of cards at nine in the evening. "I have not broken my retiring hour for Mrs. Armour," came the quick rebuff, "and I see no reason to do it for you."

Field was a cool man, but Chicago listened, quite correctly, to what he had to say. When he died in the winter of 1906 he left an estate of $120,000,000, twelve times bigger than that of Cyrus Hall McCormick, ten times bigger than that of Swift, and four times bigger than that of Armour himself.

Field had always known there was a gray charm to saving money. "As a rule," he told—of all people—Theodore Dreiser, "people do not know how to save. The average young man of today, when he begins to earn is soon inclined to habits of extravagance and wastefulness; gets somehow imbued with the idea that irrespective of what he earns, he must indulge in habits corresponding to those of some other young man, simply because he imagines that he cannot be manly without. The five, ten or fifteen cents a day that is squandered, while a mere trifle apparently, if saved would in a few years amount to thousands of dollars and go far toward establishing a future career." It was evident that he agreed with Swift that "no young man is rich enough to smoke twenty-five-cent cigars."

As for a college education, it was at best a questionable investment. "The truth is," Field enlightened Dreiser, "that for most young men a college education means that just at the time when they should be having business principles instilled into them, and be getting themselves energetically pulled together for their life's work, they are sent to college. Then intervenes what many a young man looks back on as the jolliest time of his life. . . . Often when he comes out of college this young man is unfitted by this good time to buckle down to hard work, and the result is a failure to grasp opportunities that would have opened the way for a successful career."

So much for the philosophy of the lords of Chicago. The time has come to announce the arrival in the city, on the day before Thanksgiving, 1873, of Louis Henri Sullivan, one of the great architects of the last hundred years. Sullivan lived all his life in a world far removed from that of Armour, Swift and Field. Indeed, too far removed, for the Chicago in which he believed was a city in the clouds.

In his autobiography Sullivan maintained that "the beauty, the passion, the glory of the past shall merge into a new beauty, a new passion, a new glory as man approaches man, and recognizing him, rejoices in him, and with him, as born in power." He also claimed that "never . . . has there been such sound warrant for an attitude of optimism." This does come strangely from a man who lived through the Haymarket Riot and the Pullman Strike and witnessed the campaign to defame Governor Altgeld for doing something sensible and humane in such emergencies.

Sullivan was a muddled thinker. His writings are often embarrassing. He read—or misread—volume after volume of Emerson, Herbert Spencer, Nietzsche and Veblen, and the half-digested ideas of these men reappear with alarming frequency in his vague prose. But Sullivan was after all an architect, not a writer. Although Stanford White and Augustus Saint-Gaudens could come dangerously close—as in the clock on the stairs of the Villard house in New York—to his skill as a decorator, no one has surpassed him as a designer of skyscrapers. The Guaranty Building in Buffalo and the Wainwright Building in Saint Louis remain to reprove the attempts of later generations to cope with the essence of the tall steel frame. Furthermore, he and his partner Dankmar Adler created the Auditorium.

The Auditorium has been mentioned for the second time, and not just because I should like to point out that my father, a perfect Wagnerite if ever there was one, was anxious to carry a spear in every performance he could manage of the master's works. The Auditorium has been given this emphasis because it contains—there is no point in being shy about the matter—the greatest opera house in the world in every respect: here Chicago surpasses even Paris. Its stage was dark for many years, but this was not the fault of Sullivan, but of Samuel Insull, who insisted on building a new opera house in 1929, an immense pile on the banks of the Chicago River, designed by Graham, Anderson, Probst

& White, the somewhat uninspired successors of D. H. Burnham. However, the Auditorium has now been restored, and reverently, by Harry M. Weese & Associates, and on October 31, 1967, it was reopened with the New York City Ballet's production of *A Midsummer Night's Dream*. Long before this, the hotel end of the Auditorium was given over, thanks to the generosity of the late Marshall Field III and the Julius Rosenwald Fund, to Roosevelt University.

The chief designer of this masterpiece was born in 1856 in Boston. But you must not imagine that his ties to New England were strong, or that he enjoyed as a little boy any of the security an insider had the right to demand. He was definitely an outsider. His father was a dancing-master from Ireland; his mother, a pianist from Geneva, was half Swiss-French, half German. Apparently the only strong character of Sullivan's childhood was his maternal grandfather, who took him on walks at night to contemplate the stars.

Too much has not been said about Sullivan's early years, for he remained, all his life, a prisoner of his childhood, to which two thirds of his autobiography are surrendered. His childhood came to an end the day he entered the architectural school at M.I.T., where he studied under Professor William R. Ware. To Sullivan he was no paragon; we are even told that he was "not imaginative enough to be ardent." Which may not be quite fair to this professor. He was devoted to Ruskin, as were nearly all the men who made their mark in the early annals of modern architecture. He was also the partner of Henry Van Brunt, who took the trouble to translate into English the famous *Discourses on Architecture* of Viollet-le-Duc. For Sullivan, as for Frank Lloyd Wright, Viollet-le-Duc spoke with the authority of a prophet.

Quitting M.I.T. at the end of his first year, Sullivan went on to New York, where he had a good hour or two with Richard Morris Hunt on the advantages of studying at the Ecole des Beaux Arts, and then to Philadelphia, where he talked himself into a job as a draftsman with the firm of Furness & Hewitt, doggedly committed, both partners, to the gospel of Ruskin. The Depression of 1873 put an end to his career in Philadelphia and sent him on to Chicago, where he discovered "an energy that made him tingle to be in the game." There he met William Le Baron Jenney and the rest of the crew who were to fashion the first skyscrapers.

By the summer of 1874 he was off to France, where he entered the atelier of one Emile Vaudremer at the Ecole. This experience seems to have done him no harm, in spite of the legend, still to be heard in stuffy classrooms, that the teaching at the Ecole was horridly academic. It was in Paris that he came across a tutor in mathematics by the name of Clopet who was proud of advancing demonstrations so broad as to admit of no exception. Sullivan, who was never famous for his sense of humor, was struck, fatally, by this notion. "If this can be done in mathematics, why not in architecture?" he recorded in his autobiography. "The instant answer: It can, and it shall be! *No one has*—I will!" Here no doubt was the germ of the oversimplification *Form follows function* for which Sullivan will unfortunately be remembered. In his architecture he was never dogmatic. Yet he was to strike again and again the stiff attitudes of a schoolmaster whose students have not completed their assignments. "The Master's very walk bore a dangerous resemblance to a strut," Frank Lloyd Wright has told us.

Back in Chicago, on the first of May, 1881, Sullivan became the partner of Dankmar Adler. Twelve years older than he, Adler was the rock he desperately needed. Born in Germany, the son of a rabbi who moved first to Detroit and then to Chicago, he was a formidable authority on acoustics—Carnegie Hall in New York City owes its acoustical supremacy to his advice—and a remarkable engineer. He was, Wright remembered, "one to inspire others with confidence in his power at once."

The partners could not overlook the completion in 1887 of Marshall Field's wholesale store or warehouse. The work of Henry Hobson Richardson—who brought order out of the chaos that followed the Civil War, planning Trinity Church in Boston, whose simplified massing and imperial command of granite set a standard to which architects rallied from coast to coast—the Field warehouse was the model of dignity in downtown Chicago. The lesson

was not lost on Adler & Sullivan when they began their Auditorium. Scrapping their first ambiguous elevations, they brought a new simplicity to Michigan Boulevard. In the opera house itself Sullivan spent his magnificent decorative gift on the vast elliptical arches and the golden frame for the stage. When these splendors were opened to the public on the ninth of December, 1889, and Adelina Patti rendered "Home, Sweet Home" before an audience that included the Marshall Fields and the George M. Pullmans, even President Harrison, who was not exactly renowned for his appreciation of the fine arts, was impressed. "New York surrenders, eh?" Harrison commented as he nudged the shoulder of Vice-President Levi P. Morton from the Empire State.

With such a success for the Adler & Sullivan office, the younger partner could look with equanimity at the work of his competitors. He had, however, to respect the work of Burnham & Root, who were responsible for the Richardsonian grandeurs of the Rookery, the Woman's Temple and the Masonic Temple, three of the unforgettable skyscrapers, and for the Monadnock Building. This last, which made use of masonry bearing walls rather than the steel-frame method of construction, was alleged to be the work of Root alone. It was bare of all ornament, a monument to the investment in Chicago real estate of the trustees of the fortune of Henry Adams' grandfather, Peter Chardon Brooks of Boston.

"My idea," Burnham said to Sullivan, "is to work up a big big business, to handle big things, deal with big businessmen, and to build up a big organization, for you can't handle big things unless you have an organization." Sullivan had now met the man who was qualified as was no one else to face Chicago head on. "He was elephantine, tactless and blurting," the designer of the Auditorium recalled. "He got many a humiliating knock on the nose in his quest of the big; but he faltered not—his purpose was fixed. Himself not especially susceptible to flattery except in a sentimental way, he soon learned its efficacy when plastered thick on big businessmen." But this was also the man who turned to Sullivan one evening and said: "See! Louis, how beautiful the moon is now, overhead, how tender. Something in her beauty suggests tears to me."

As for Root, he too was a personality. "He was not of Burnham's type," Sullivan reported, "but . . . a man of quick-witted all-around culture which he carried easily and jauntily, and vain to the limit of the skies. . . . His temperament was that of the well-groomed free-lance, never taking anything too seriously, wherein he differed from his ponderous partner, much as dragon-fly and mastiff. Nor had he one tenth of his partner's settled will, nor of said partner's capacity to go through hell to reach an end. John Root's immediate ambition was to shine."

In the meantime, enterprising Chicagoans were descending on Washington to plead the city's right to be the site of a World's Fair honoring the 400th anniversary of the discovery of America, and the day came when the House of Representatives agreed. The buildings were to be dedicated in 1892, and the Fair itself to open for six months beginning May 1, 1893. To Root this was Chicago's chance to rival the recent expositions in Paris. "We have more space, more money, and we have the lake," he commented. "Why should we not surpass Paris?" He died of pneumonia early in 1891 while the Fair was still in the early stages, but had already reported to the Committee on Grounds and Buildings that "it would be wise to select a certain number of architects because of their prominence in the profession, choosing each man for such work as would be most parallel with his best achievements." What this meant was that Burnham & Root, as administrators, would design no buildings themselves for the Fair, and that Chicago would be informed by the last word from the East.

A revolution, no less, had recently taken place in New York, where in 1881 Richard Morris Hunt hit on the happy idea of building a palace in Caen limestone in the manner of the early French Renaissance for Mr. and Mrs. W. K. Vanderbilt. After years of searching, Hunt had arrived at the perfect formula for a millionaire's town house: his success was made more than evident when the Vanderbilts humbled the Astors on the evening of March 26, 1883, by giving in their new and noble château the grandest party in the history of Manhattan Island.

This rediscovery of the Renaissance and its charms could not be ignored by Hunt's rivals. Suddenly the firm of McKim, Mead & White, who had gone a long way on the road to modern architecture in the informal shingle-style houses they had been contriving for Newport and other summer resorts, made an about-face. The complex of five adjoining houses they created in 1885 for the railroad magnate Henry Villard and four of his friends—still standing, these houses, to the rear of St. Patrick's Cathedral—indicated that they would be henceforth as dedicated to the ideals of the Renaissance as Hunt himself. That strange thing called taste had changed. The change was almost immediately noted in Chicago, where Hunt in 1884 provided a château very like that of the W. K. Vanderbilts for the William Bordens. The Bordens could not be said to draw upon the unlimited resources of the Vanderbilts, but William's father had recently amassed something like $2,300,000 by joining Marshall Field in buying up a silver mine or two at Leadville, Colorado.

There was no public protest when the Bordens moved into their new house on Lake Shore Drive, and you might suppose that there would be no protest over inviting Richard Morris Hunt, McKim, Mead & White and a few other distinguished firms from the East to contribute to the Fair. A protest, however, was made, and the fiercest controversy in the history of American architecture is still raging over the lagoons that graced Jackson Park in the summer of 1893.

The reasons for the controversy, ancient though it may be, are worth looking into. First of all, the Fair was a tremendous success. Four hundred thousand people poured through the turnstiles on the opening day, and Ward McAllister showed a genuine concern over the hearty hospitality promised Easterners by Mayor Carter H. Harrison. "I may say," McAllister announced, "that it is not quantity but quality that society people want. Hospitality which includes the whole human race is not desirable."

Secondly, a number of foolish statements about the Fair were made by men who should have known better. The sculptor Saint-Gaudens, for example, revealed that he was a member in good standing of what must be called a mutual-admiration society. "Look here, old fellow," he called out at the end of a conference attended by Hunt and McKim, "do you realize that this is the greatest meeting of artists since the fifteenth century?" And it must be admitted that Burnham was a trifle too apologetic when face to face with the great men of the East: his name cannot be dropped from the list of those who have made their contribution to the history of Chicago's famous inferiority complex. "We have been in an inventive period, and have had rather a contempt for the classics," he suggested. "Men evolved new ideas and imagined they could start a new school without much reference to the past." A little of this sort of thing went a long way with Hunt, who was certain to explode at the slightest hint of the cultural inferiority of the city in which he found himself. "Hell," he broke into one of Burnham's discourses, "we haven't come out here on a missionary expedition. Let's get down to work."

By now we have nearly everything that was needed to start the controversy over the Fair. Things were going very well indeed, so well that a little resentment would be natural, particularly on the part of those who realized that Saint-Gaudens could be pompous at times, and sensed that Burnham had sold Chicago short in running down his own early work. For tempers to snap, there was only one thing missing, and it was not missing for long. This was the entrance upon the scene of those curious people (some of them are still with us today) who believed that modern architecture was a tender flower, very like an orchid, which might fade away if set in the shade of a building in the Renaissance manner.

It is interesting that Sullivan does not seem to have belonged to this group in 1893. He had, of course, no reason to. He was not slighted, not in the least. He and Henry Ives Cobb (whose Fisheries Building was a thing in the Richardsonian style) had been selected to represent the Chicago point of view. Moreover, Sullivan's Transportation Building, the salient feature of which was a gorgeously deco-rated golden doorway, was, in the opinion of many people, the outstanding exhibit of the art of architecture at the Fair. In any event, he was the only architect to be recognized in Europe: in the next year he received three medals from the Union Centrale des Arts Décoratifs.

As for the exhibits of Hunt and of McKim, Mead & White, neither the former's Administration Building nor the latter's Agricultural Building added a single leaf to their laurels. Better things had been done before by Hunt and McKim, Mead & White; better things would be done in the future. While it is true that the sight of these classic façades sent Henry Adams into ecstasy, he seems to have been less excited by their beauty than by the claims that might now be advanced for the social position of artists and intellectuals in the United States. "Chicago," he said, referring to the Fair, "was the first expression of American thought as a unity." This was bunk. "If," he went on, "the people of the Northwest actually knew what was good when they saw it, they would some day talk about Hunt and Richardson, La Farge and Saint-Gaudens, Burnham and McKim and Stanford White, when their politicians and millionaires were otherwise forgotten."

A shrewder estimate of the Fair as a whole was made by the leading architectural critic of the day, Montgomery Schuyler. "Arcadian architecture is one thing and American architecture another," he declared. "Men bring not back the mastodons nor we those times."

But to return to Sullivan. The business of Adler & Sullivan, like that of many other firms, declined in the wake of the depression of 1893, and on the eleventh of July, 1895, Adler decided he must retire from the practice of architecture to become consulting architect and general sales manager of the Crane Elevator Company. For Sullivan this was a blow from which he never recovered. His genius, of course, was never to fail him, but without Adler's business sense to guide him, he was a lost man. On his own (with the assistance of his faithful associate George Elmslie) he was to design the marvelously ornamented department store of Schlesinger & Mayer, now occupied by Carson, Pirie Scott & Co., though he could never hope to be as subtle as Louis Sullivan.

Who knows, such a thought may even have come to Frank Lloyd Wright early in his career on his way home to Oak Park. He was always a man of uncommon sense, and was never shrewder than when he settled in the suburb Ernest Hemingway was to run away from. The affluence of the North Shore, where temperatures, thanks to the lake, range from ten to fifteen degrees cooler on summer days, was not Wright's to command. But in the more modest surroundings of Oak Park the commandments of Armour, Swift and Field might be less distinctly heard. Life in a western suburb might be less expensive than in Winnetka or Lake Forest. It could also be less orthodox.

This is not to say that Wright fled for a second the tension that was ever in the air of Chicago.

Tensions may intimidate weak artists but strengthen the strong, as Friedrich Nietzsche understood when he wrote that "art alone is what keeps the bow from snapping."

It may be too soon in 1968 to measure what has been determined, dared and done since the deaths of Eliel and Eero Saarinen and Frank Lloyd Wright, but it is obvious that the Middle West continues to be an attractive terrain to architects answering questions that have not yet been asked. No one can predict, for example, what surprises a firm like Meathe, Kessler & Associates may have planned for tomorrow.

In any event, it is a happy fact and not a boast that in the last hundred years no nation in the world has matched the architecture of Chicago and the Middle West.

In Memoriam D. H. Burnham: The lakefront in the summer of 1967.

CONTENTS

POCKETS OF RESISTANCE 1–6

THE ROMANTIC YEARS, 7–14

"THINGS VERY ANCIENT NEVER, FOR SOME MYSTERIOUS REASON, APPEAR VULGAR," 15–22

HENRY HOBSON RICHARDSON, 23–25

WILSON EYRE, JR., 26

HENRY IVES COBB, 27–29

PEABODY & STEARNS, 30

HARVEY ELLIS, 31–33

SOLON SPENCER BEMAN, 34–35

WILLIAM LE BARON JENNEY, 36–37

HOLABIRD & ROCHE, 38–39

BURNHAM & ROOT, 40–43

D. H. BURNHAM & CO., 44

LOUIS H. SULLIVAN, 45–60

THE WORLD'S FAIR OF 1893, 61–64

THE EARLY WORK OF FRANK LLOYD WRIGHT, 65–84

THE CHICAGO SCHOOL, 85–106

ALDEN B. DOW, 107

ECLECTICS IN THE MIDDLE WEST, 108–119

THE RETURN OF FRANK LLOYD WRIGHT, 120–140

ALBERT KAHN, 141–145

ELIEL SAARINEN, 146–149

ELIEL AND EERO SAARINEN, 150–151

EERO SAARINEN, 152–158

LUDWIG MIËS VAN DER ROHE, 159–169

SKIDMORE, OWINGS & MERRILL, 170–171

MINORU YAMASAKI, 172

MARCEL BREUER, 173

RALPH RAPSON/BERTRAND GOLDBERG, 174

HARRY M. WEESE, 175

R. BUCKMINSTER FULLER, 176–177

MEATHE, KESSLER & ASSOCIATES, 178–179

BIBLIOGRAPHY

INDEX

Capital from the Mormon Temple at Nauvoo, Illinois, 1841–46 (architect un-
known). Elder William Weeks was retained as "architect," but whether he was
more than a draftsman who took orders from Joseph Smith remains to be proved.
Arsonists burned the temple to the ground in 1848; a mate to this capital from
Nauvoo may be seen on the grounds of the Historical Society at Quincy. The
prophet Joseph Smith and his brother Hyrum were murdered by the mob that
assailed the jail at Carthage, Illinois, on June 27, 1844.

The Middle West has yet to apply for the copyright on conformity. There have
always been pockets of resistance to prevailing opinions. The Mormons provided
an early example. So did the founders of the utopian communities of New
Harmony, Bishop Hill and Zoar.

*Mormon Temple, Kirtland, Ohio, 1833–36 (architect unknown). The Mormons
tarried in Ohio before descending on Commerce, Illinois, and renaming it Nauvoo.*

*Two views of the residence of David Dale Owen,
New Harmony, Indiana, 1859 (David Dale Owen
and James Renwick, Jr.). New Harmony was
first settled by George Rapp and his fellow
pietists, who fled Württemberg to establish a
religious community in the New World free
from the threat of official dogmatism. In 1825
the lands were sold to Robert Owen, the British
mill-owner, who saw here the chance to build a
socialist utopia. His son David Dale Owen, a
geologist who was the first to emphasize the
mineral resources of Iowa and Wisconsin, called
on Renwick, the architect of Grace Church, New
York, for assistance in designing this Gothic
Revival dwelling. Robert Dale Owen, David's
brother, publicized Renwick's plan for the
Smithsonian Institution in Washington.*

Roofless Church, New Harmony, Indiana, 1960 (Philip C. Johnson). Complete with a sculpture by Jacques Lipchitz, this church was erected in memory of the sacrifices of the Rappites and Owenites.

OPPOSITE ABOVE: *Steeple Building, Bishop Hill, Illinois, 1854 (architect unknown).* BELOW: *Communal housing, Bishop Hill, Illinois, 1854 (architect unknown). Bishop Hill was the creation of Swedish pietists led by Olaf Olson.*

4

Number One House, Zoar, Ohio, 1835 (architect unknown). Zoar was built by the followers of Joseph Bäumeler, a German separatist who brought his colony to America in 1817. Number One House, recalling the architecture of the eighteenth century on the Eastern Seaboard, was originally intended to house the aged. It became Bäumeler's own headquarters.

The romantic years—from 1830 to 1860—witnessed in the Middle West as elsewhere in America the expansion of the Greek and Gothic Revivals, both of which had been introduced in 1799 to Philadelphia by Benjamin Henry Latrobe, chief architect of the Capitol in Washington.

Residence of Dr. Andrew L. Hays, Marshall, Michigan, c. 1838 (architect unknown). This may be the finest Greek Revival mansion in Michigan.

ABOVE: *The Elms, Hudson, Ohio, 1850–53 (Simeon Porter?).*

BELOW: *Honolulu House, residence of Abner Platt, Marshall, Michigan, 1860 (architect unknown). The Elms gives some indication of the range of Gothic fantasy in the Middle West. Platt's bracketed Italian villa, following yet another popular style in the romantic years, may have been inspired by the work of Henry Austin around New Haven, Connecticut. Platt had been consul in the Hawaiian Islands.*

Hillforest, residence of Thomas Gaff, Aurora, Indiana, 1852–56 (architect unknown). Today the headquarters of the Hillforest Historical Foundation, this house could have been suggested by the Regency style in early nineteenth-century England.

ABOVE: *Saint James Church, Grosse Ile, Michigan, 1867 (Gordon W. Lloyd).*
BELOW: *Mitchell-Turner house, Milan, Ohio, 1847–48 (architect unknown).*

*Residence of John S. Moffat, Hudson, Wisconsin, c. 1865 (architect unknown).
In 1968 the headquarters of the Saint Croix Valley Historical Society, the Moffat
house is an excellent Midwestern example of the octagon style, popularized in the
1850s by Orson Squire Fowler and his brother Lorenzo. Fowler had been famous
as a phrenologist before he turned his attention to the* home for all, *as he called
his octagons.*

ABOVE: *Residence of Charles H. Lewis, Hudson, Wisconsin, c. 1865 (architect unknown).* BELOW: *Residence of J. Russell Jones, Galena, Illinois, 1857 (architect unknown). For those who shied away from Gothic cottages, there was always the Italian villa, of which style the Jones house may be the best example in Illinois.*

ABOVE: *Residence of John M. Wheeler, Ann Arbor, Michigan, c. 1851 (architect unknown).* BELOW: *Old State Bank, Shawneetown, Illinois, 1839 (architect unknown). The Gothic specimen from Ann Arbor has been now altered out of recognition, but the Grecian temple in southern Illinois has survived.*

Doorway, the Avery-Downer house, Granville, Ohio, 1838–42
(Benjamin Morgan).

Residence of Benjamin Franklin Allen, Des Moines, Iowa, 1869 (W. W. Boyington). There may be no more dramatic example in the United States of the mansardic style so popular in the 1860s and 1870s. Allen was a banker who went bankrupt.

"Things very ancient never, for some mysterious reason, appear vulgar," wrote Henry James on contemplating the mansion of Jacques Coeur at Bourges. This comment could be made also about many an American monument in the hectic years following the Civil War.

Two views of the Chicago Water Tower, Michigan Avenue at Chicago Avenue, Chicago, Illinois, 1869 (W. W. Boyington). The Water Tower, which miraculously survived the Great Chicago Fire, is a building dear to all Chicagoans. It was guilty of amusing Oscar Wilde on his inspection of the city in 1883.

Van Wert County Courthouse, Van Wert, Ohio, 1875–76 (Thomas J. Tolan). Aesthetes may shudder, but it is a fact that most great monuments are memorials to ambition. There may be no more ambitious courthouse in America than this mansardic example.

17

ABOVE: *Eads Bridge, Saint Louis, Missouri, 1867–74 (James Buchanan Eads)*. BELOW: *Pillsbury "A" Mill, Minneapolis, Minnesota, 1880 (L. S. Buffington). Eads was an engineer who remains a legendary figure to all architects. Buffington was an architect who will never be forgotten by architectural historians: he claimed to have invented the skyscraper, but his patent was proved fraudulent by Professor Dimitri Tselos. The dates on the pertinent drawings were faked.*

The Chicago Historical Society

The Chicago Historical Society

ABOVE: *The Palmer House, Chicago, Illinois, 1873 (John Mills Van Osdel).* BELOW: *The Palmer House dining room. Now replaced by the hotel bearing the same name, this was the second Palmer House to be seen on State Street: it replaced the original, which disappeared in the Great Chicago Fire. The owner, Marshall Field's former partner Potter Palmer, found that Cyrus Hall McCormick was a difficult guest in the dining room. The inventor of the reaper insisted on a cut rate for dinner. Said Palmer to McCormick, fearing that the news might spread: "The price that we agreed upon for dinners I wish confined to yourself only, for the reason that 75 cents does not pay me the actual cost of dinners."*

The Chicago Historical Society

The Chicago Architectural Photographing Co.

Marshall Field Wholesale Store or Warehouse, Chicago, Illinois, 1885–87. Now demolished, this building, which stood on the block bounded by Wells, Franklin, Quincy and Adams Streets, haunted Louis Sullivan and many another Chicago architect. Richardson died with Field's name on his lips, whispering to the doctor that he longed "to live two years to see the Pittsburgh Court House and the Chicago store complete." On those two works he felt his reputation would stand.

OPPOSITE ABOVE: *Residence of Marshall Field, 1905 Prairie Avenue, Chicago, Illinois, 1873 (Richard Morris Hunt).* BELOW: *Residence of William Borden, 1020 Lake Shore Drive, Chicago, Illinois, 1884 (Richard Morris Hunt). Both these mansions have been demolished. When Marshall Field gave a party in 1885 for his son Marshall Field II and his daughter Ethel (later the wife of Admiral Beatty), the favors were designed in London by none other than James McNeill Whistler. It was in the Borden castle that Adlai E. Stevenson courted his wife, William Borden's granddaughter.*

ABOVE: *Residence of Franklin MacVeagh, Chicago, Illinois, 1885–87.* BELOW: *Residence of John J. Glessner, 1800 Prairie Avenue, Chicago, Illinois, 1885–87. The MacVeagh house, now destroyed, was the fortress on Lake Shore Drive of the wholesale groceries dealer who became Taft's Secretary of the Treasury. The Glessner house, occupied in 1968 by the Chicago School of Architecture Foundation, was the monument of a pioneer in the farm machinery business; his concern, like that of McCormick, was ultimately merged in International Harvester.*

Doorway, residence of John J. Glessner, 1800 Prairie Avenue, Chicago, Illinois, 1885–87.

Residence of Charles Lang Freer, 71 East Ferry Avenue, Detroit, Michigan, c. 1887. The finest example in the Middle West of the so-called shingle style popularized by McKim, Mead & White at Newport, the Freer house serves in 1968 as headquarters of the Merrill-Palmer Institute for training teachers for young children. Freer, who made his money building railroad cars, was the friend and patron of James McNeill Whistler. Here, in an annex, was stored Whistler's Peacock Room before it was removed to the Freer Gallery in Washington.

ABOVE: *Presbyterian Church, Lake Forest, Illinois, 1886.* BELOW: *Former Chicago Historical Society Building, northwest corner of Dearborn and Ontario Streets, Chicago, Illinois, 1892.*

A devoted Richardsonian when he designed the Chicago Historical Society and the Newberry Library nearby, Cobb eventually turned to a somewhat scholarly version of the Gothic for the early buildings of the University of Chicago.

Residence of Clement Studebaker, 600 West Washington Street, South Bend, Indiana, 1886. This wagon manufacturer was known to have entertained Presidents Grant, Harrison and McKinley.

Cobb's partner in the design of this Richardsonian landmark and of the Palmer residence was Charles S. Frost.

Residence of Potter Palmer, Lake Shore Drive at Banks Street, Chicago, Illinois, 1882. "The age of Pericles seems to be dawning in Chicago," the Inter-Ocean saluted this angry Gothic castle. Boni de Castellane, who called on Mrs. Palmer before his marriage to Jay Gould's daughter, was not so easily pleased. On penetrating the porte-cochère, he pronounced the castle "sumptuous and abominable." It is now demolished.

Residence of James J. Hill, 240 Summit Avenue, Saint Paul, Minnesota, 1891. Although Hill chose an Eastern firm to design his mansion (in 1968 occupied by the Archdiocese), he never lost sight of the importance of Chicago. In Chicago he never failed to call on Marshall Field. "He has the damndest eyes," the master of the Great Northern Railroad told Field's nephew. "I go in there to ask him a question, and by the time I've come out, I've told him all I know. He pumps me dry."

Doorway, Mabel Tainter Memorial, Menomonie, Wisconsin, 1889. This community center was built in honor of the daughter of the local lumber magnate Andrew Tainter. Harvey Ellis was a marvelous draftsman and an incorrigible alcoholic. This meant that his talent was spent not on his own fame but on that of the firms for which he worked, and not until a careful examination has been made of the production of J. Walter Stevens in Saint Paul, L. S. Buffington in Minneapolis, and Eckel & Mann in Saint Louis and Saint Joseph, Missouri, may his exact contribution be defined. Just such an examination is being made by Roger G. Kennedy. It seems certain, however, in 1968 that Ellis was the author not only of the Tainter Memorial but also of the Motter and McAllister houses in Saint Joseph and Washington Terrace in Saint Louis.

ABOVE: *Mabel Tainter Memorial, Menomonie, Wisconsin, 1889.* BELOW: *Doorway, residence of Joshua Motter, Saint Joseph, Missouri, 1890.*

32

ABOVE: *Residence of James W. McAllister, Saint Joseph, Missouri, 1890.* BELOW: *Detail, gates to Washington Terrace, Saint Louis, Missouri, 1893.*

Hotel Florence, Pullman, Illinois, 1881. Named for Pullman's daughter, later the wife of Governor Lowden.

The failings of the model town were exposed during the Pullman strike of 1894. "The damned idiot ought to arbitrate, arbitrate and arbitrate!" roared that eminent and sensible Republican Mark Hanna. A friend spoke of all the fine things Pullman had done for his workmen in the model town. "Oh, hell!" said Hanna. "Model ——! Go and live in Pullman and find out how much Pullman gets sellin' city water and gas to those poor fools! . . . A man who won't meet his own men halfway is a God-damn fool!" When Pullman died in the fall of 1897, leaving an estate of $17,400,000, his family, perhaps because they feared reprisals from wayward employees, buried him with care, embedding his coffin in asphalt and binding it down by steel rails through which no ghoul could hope to claw. In 1968 the Pullman plant has been abandoned by the Pullman Co.

OPPOSITE ABOVE: *Pullman Works, Pullman, Illinois, 1881.* BELOW: *Pullman housing, Pullman, Illinois, 1881.*

Assisted by I. K. Pond, Beman was responsible for the model town on the South Side constructed by the inventor of the lower and upper berths.

The Chicago Architectural Photographing Co.

Home Insurance Building, southwest corner of LaSalle and Adams Streets, Chi-
cago, Illinois, 1883. This candidate for the distinction of being the world's first
skyscraper was erected during the decade in which Loop property soared from
$130,000 the quarter-acre to $900,000. The Home Insurance has been demolished.

36

Leiter Building I, northwest corner of Wells and Monroe Streets, Chicago, Illinois, 1879. As Carl Condit has pointed out, the First Leiter is very nearly a glass box. Although its brick piers are not essential bearing members, the outer floor beams are carried over to iron columns immediately inside the piers, which means the latter are freed from interior loads, making possible something resembling a glass envelope. Leiter I was originally five stories high; two more were added in 1888.

The Chicago Architectural Photographing Co.

Tacoma Building, northeast corner of La Salle and Madison Streets, Chicago, Illinois, 1886–89. This second candidate for the distinction of being the first skyscraper was the first whose structural frame was riveted. Now demolished.

LEFT: *The Monroe Building, southwest corner of Monroe Street and Michigan Avenue, Chicago, Illinois, 1912.* RIGHT: *The University Club, northwest corner of Monroe Street and Michigan Avenue, Chicago, Illinois, 1909. Although damned as "eclectic" by architectural historians who bristle at the slightest evidence of historicism, these skyscrapers remain an elegant addition to the Chicago skyline.*

The Chicago Architectural Photographing Co.

40

*The Monadnock Building, 53 West Jackson Boulevard, Chicago, Illinois, 1891–93.
Root's first sketches were rejected as too ornate; in his absence Burnham suggested
an uncompromising, unornamented façade. With this scheme Root in the end
grandly agreed.*

The Chicago Architectural Photographing Co.

Woman's Temple, southwest corner of La Salle and Monroe Streets, Chicago, Illinois, 1891–92. This skyscraper, commissioned by the Women's Christian Temperance Union, has been demolished.

ABOVE: *Masonic Temple (originally The Capitol Building), northwest corner of State and Randolph Streets, Chicago, Illinois, 1891–92. Now demolished, this twenty-two-story structure was the highest building in the world at the time.* BELOW: *Entrance to Rookery Building, 209 South La Salle Street, Chicago, Illinois, 1886–88. The lobby was remodeled by Frank Lloyd Wright in 1905 (see page 67).*

Reliance Building, 32 North State Street, Chicago, Illinois, 1890–94. The design-ing architect was neither Burnham nor Root but Charles B. Atwood, whose ec-lectic Art Building at the Fair may be seen on page 63.

D. H. BURNHAM & CO.

Railway Exchange Building, northwest corner of Michigan Avenue and Jackson Boulevard, Chicago, Illinois 1903–04. In an office atop this skyscraper, a superb example of what Burnham could accomplish without Root, the Chicago Plan was conceived.

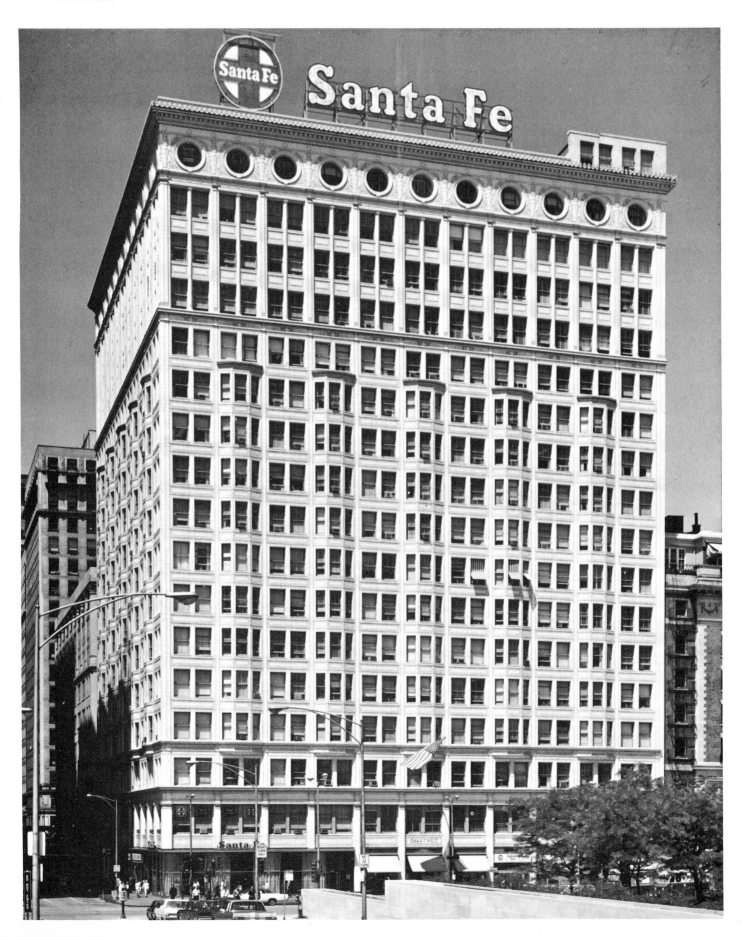

ABOVE: *Detail, Congress Street façade, The Auditorium, Michigan Avenue at Congress Street, Chicago, Illinois, 1887–89.* BELOW: *The Auditorium from across Michigan Avenue.*

45

The Auditorium, to the right of the stage (as restored by Harry M. Weese).

46

Frame of the stage of the Auditorium (as restored by Harry M. Weese).

*Schiller Building, later the Garrick Theatre Building, 64 West Randolph Street,
Chicago, Illinois, 1891–92. In the foreground is the Borden Block, the work of
Dankmar Adler & Co., 1879–80. Both buildings have been demolished.*

Richard Nickel

Interior of the theater in the Schiller Building.

ABOVE: *Tomb of Martin Ryerson, Graceland Cemetery, Chicago, Illinois, 1889.*
BELOW: *Tomb of Charlotte Dickson Wainwright, Bellefontaine Cemetery, Saint Louis, Missouri, 1892. Martin Ryerson—no relation of the E. L. Ryerson whose mansion in Lake Forest may be seen on page 110—was the father of the Martin A. Ryerson who gave so many Renoirs to the Art Institute of Chicago. Charlotte Dickson Wainwright was the wife of the brewer for whom Sullivan built the Wainwright Building (opposite).*

Richard Nickel

Wainwright Building, northwest corner of Seventh and Chestnut Streets, Saint Louis, Missouri, 1890–91.

Tomb of Carrie Eliza Getty, Graceland Cemetery, Chicago, Illinois, 1890.

ABOVE: *Entrance to Stock Exchange Building, 30 North La Salle Street, Chicago, Illinois, 1894.* BELOW: *People's Savings & Loan Association Building, southeast corner of Court Street and Ohio Avenue, Sidney, Ohio, 1917–18.*

Richard Nickel

Schlesinger & Mayer Department Store, southeast corner of State and Madison Streets, Chicago, Illinois, 1899–1904. Now occupied by Carson, Pirie Scott & Co. Original cornice removed.

Detail, entrance, Schlesinger & Mayer store. George Elmslie was responsible for the ornament in this instance.

ABOVE: *Merchants National Bank (later Poweshiek County National Bank), northwest corner, Fourth Avenue and Broad Street, Grinnell, Iowa, 1914.* BELOW: *Farmers & Merchants Union Bank, northwest corner, James Street and Broadway, Columbus, Wisconsin, 1919.*

56

National Farmers Bank, northeast corner, Broadway and Cedar Streets, Owatonna, Minnesota, 1908. George Elmslie was partly responsible for this design.

ABOVE: *Detail, façade of the National Farmers Bank.* BELOW: *Interior. On the right may be seen part of the restoration and enlargement by Harwell Hamilton Harris in 1958.*

ABOVE: *Residence of Henry Babson, Riverside, Illinois, 1907.* BELOW: *Residence of Josephine Crane Bradley, 106 North Prospect Street, Madison, Wisconsin, 1909. The Babson house has been destroyed. The Bradley house in 1968 is the Sigma Phi Fraternity House.*

59

William P. Krause Music Store and residence, 4611 North Lincoln Avenue, Chicago, Illinois, 1922. In 1968 the Arntzen-Coleman Funeral Home.

The Chicago Historical Society

Administration Building (Richard Morris Hunt).

ABOVE: *Agricultural Building (McKim, Mead & White).* BELOW: *Manufactures Building (George B. Post).*

ABOVE: *Fisheries Building (Henry Ives Cobb).* BELOW: *Art Building (Charles B. Atwood). Resurfaced and recarved in limestone, the Art Building survives in 1968 as the Museum of Science and Industry in Jackson Park.*

Transportation Building (Louis H. Sullivan). The Golden Doorway was not wholly original, as Professor Dimitri Tselos has recently proved. A possible precedent may be found in the Auguenaou Gate in Marrakech, Morocco.

OPPOSITE ABOVE: *Residence of George Blossom, Chicago, Illinois, 1892.* BELOW: *Residence of Isidor Heller, Chicago, Illinois, 1897.*

Residence of W. H. Winslow, River Forest, Illinois, 1893.

OPPOSITE ABOVE: *Lobby of the Rookery, 209 South La Salle Street, Chicago, Illinois, 1905. (A view of the entrance is on page 42.)* BELOW: *Residence of James Charnley, Chicago, Illinois, 1891. Although attributed to Adler & Sullivan, there is every reason to believe that this is the work of Wright. Originally the house was symmetrical; the extreme right is an addition.*

67

Residence of Ward W. Willitts, Highland Park, Illinois, 1902.

OPPOSITE ABOVE: *Side view, Unitarian Universalist Church (Unity Temple), Lake Street at Kenilworth Avenue, Oak Park, Illinois, 1906.* BELOW: *Interior.*

Front view, Unitarian Universalist Church (Unity Temple), Lake Street at Kenilworth Avenue, Oak Park, Illinois, 1906.

OPPOSITE ABOVE: *Residence of F. F. Tomek, Riverside, Illinois, 1907.* BELOW: *Residence of Isabel Roberts, River Forest, Illinois, 1908.*

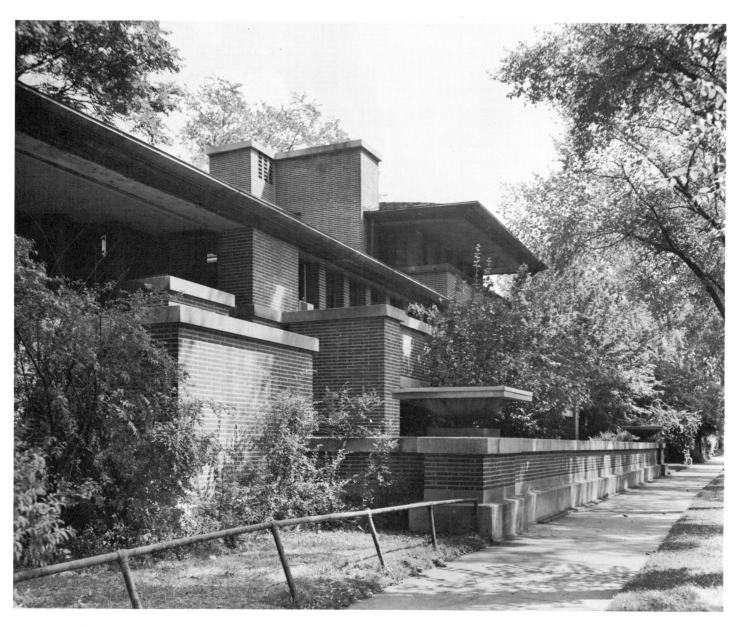

Residence of Frederick C. Robie, Chicago, Illinois, 1909.

ABOVE: *Residence of P. A. Beachy, Oak Park, Illinois, 1906.* BELOW: *Residence of W. G. Fricke, Oak Park, Illinois, 1902.*

Residence of Thomas P. Hardy, Racine, Wisconsin, 1905.

OPPOSITE ABOVE: *Residence of W. E. Martin, Oak Park, Illinois, 1903.* BELOW: *Residence of Emil Balch, Chicago, Illinois, 1915.*

Residence of B. Harley Bradley, Kankakee, Illinois, 1900.

ABOVE: *Residence of Francis W. Little, Peoria, Illinois, 1903.* BELOW: *Residence of Warren Hickox, Kankakee, Illinois, 1900.*

Residence of Avery Coonley, Riverside, Illinois, 1908. The Coonley house has now been altered beyond recognition.

OPPOSITE ABOVE: *Living room, residence of Avery Coonley.* BELOW: *Playhouse for residence of Avery Coonley, Riverside, Illinois, 1912. The Coonley playhouse has also been altered.*

The Chicago Architectural Photographing Co.

ABOVE: *Residence of E. H. Cheney, Oak Park, Illinois, 1904.* BELOW: *Residence of Susan L. Dana, Springfield, Illinois, 1903.*

Midway Gardens, Cottage Grove Avenue at 60th Street, Chicago, Illinois, 1914. Demolished.

ABOVE: *Residence of Mayer May, Grand Rapids, Michigan, 1909.* BELOW: *Residence of E. A. Gilmore, Madison, Wisconsin, 1908.*

82

Studio, Taliesin East, residence of Frank Lloyd Wright, Spring Green, Wisconsin, 1925–1959.

ABOVE: *Far view, Taliesin East, residence of Frank Lloyd Wright, Spring Green, Wisconsin, 1925–1959.* BELOW: *Entrance.*

84

ABOVE: *Entrance, Carl Schurz High School, northeast corner of Milwaukee and Addison Avenues, Chicago, Illinois, 1909 (Dwight H. Perkins).* BELOW: *Side view. A graduate of the office of Burnham & Root, Perkins became the chief architect of the Chicago Board of Education.*

Chapin & Gore Building, 63 East Adams Street, Chicago, Illinois, 1904 (Hugh
M. G. Garden in the office of Richard E. Schmidt). The Canadian Hugh M. G.
Garden was to join the Bavarian-born Richard E. Schmidt and the structural
engineer Edgar Martin to form the firm of Schmidt, Garden & Martin in 1906.
The Chapin & Gore Building has been altered since this photograph was taken.

ABOVE: *Montgomery Ward Warehouse, 618 West Chicago Avenue, Chicago, Illinois, 1907 (Schmidt, Garden & Martin). This is the largest building of the Chicago School to be supported on a reinforced concrete frame.* BELOW: *Residence of Albert F. Madlener, Chicago, Illinois, 1902 (Richard E. Schmidt).*

Residence of Robert Herrick, Chicago, Illinois, 1900 (Hugh M. G. Garden).
Herrick, who taught at the University of Chicago, was the author of one of the
superior Chicago novels, Memoirs of an American Citizen.

ABOVE: *Residence of Robert Mueller, Decatur, Illinois, 1910 (Marion Mahony and Hermann von Holst).* BELOW: *Residence of J. H. Amberg, Grand Rapids, Michigan, 1910 (Marion Mahony and Hermann von Holst). Marion Mahony, perhaps the most gifted draftsman on Wright's staff, was to become the wife of Walter Burley Griffin. To her and Von Holst, Wright entrusted these and other commissions in the office when he and Mamah Borthwick Cheney (the Cheney house is shown on page 80) set off for Europe, abandoning the Wright and Cheney households in Oak Park.*

Residence of J. G. Melson, Mason City, Iowa, 1913 (Walter Burley Griffin).
Griffin, another of Wright's assistants, won the international competition for the
planning of Canberra, the capital of Australia, and spent the rest of his life there
and in India.

OPPOSITE ABOVE: *Residence for Hurd Comstock, Evanston, Illinois, 1912 (Walter*
Burley Griffin). BELOW: *Residence of Harry Page, Mason City, Iowa, 1913*
(Walter Burley Griffin).

Stinson Library, Anna, Illinois, 1914 (Walter Burley Griffin).

Residence of J. F. Clarke, Fairfield, Iowa, 1915 (Barry Byrne). Yet another graduate of the Wright office, Byrne was later to make his reputation as the architect of many Roman Catholic churches.

Residence of George W. Maher, Kenilworth, Illinois, 1893 (George W. Maher).

OPPOSITE ABOVE: *Joseph Sears School, Kenilworth, Illinois, 1912 (George W. Maher).* BELOW: *Kenilworth Club, Kenilworth, Illinois, 1907 (George W. Maher). Maher, who worked in the office of J. L. Silsbee at Wright's side before the latter joined Adler & Sullivan, was most respected for the boulder-hewn residence of the grain speculator James A. Patten in Evanston, Illinois, and for the Patten Gymnasium given to Northwestern University. Both of these buildings in Evanston have been destroyed.*

Winona Savings Bank, Winona, Minnesota, 1916 (George W. Maher). Here Maher seems to have been tempted by the classic revival advocated by Burnham.

Residence of J. Hall Taylor, Oak Park, Illinois, 1913 (George W. Maher).

Brookfield Kindergarten, Brookfield, Illinois, c. 1912 (Guenzel & Drummond). Louis Guenzel was a German who got his start in the office of Adler & Sullivan. His partner, William Drummond, was once one of Wright's assistants. Together they designed this kindergarten (since converted to a private residence) for one of Mrs. Avery Coonley's experiments in children's education.

OPPOSITE ABOVE: *First Congregational Church of Austin (in 1968 Our Lady of Lebanon Church), 5701 West Midway Park Avenue, Chicago, Illinois, 1908 (Guenzel & Drummond).* BELOW: *Thorncroft, Riverside, Illinois, 1912 (Guenzel & Drummond). This building was erected to house teachers Mrs. Coonley engaged.*

Women's Club, 526 Ashland Avenue, River Forest, Illinois, 1913 (Guenzel & Drummond).

Woodbury County Courthouse, corner of Seventh and Douglas Streets, Sioux City, Iowa, 1915–17 (Purcell & Elmslie in association with William L. Steele). The firm of Purcell & Elmslie (or Purcell, Feick & Elmslie as it was known from 1909 to 1913 when George Feick was also a partner) was steeped as was no other in the tradition of Louis Sullivan. William Gray Purcell had served in Sullivan's office before joining that of John Galen Howard in Berkeley, California. George Grant Elmslie, with Adler & Sullivan at the time Wright came to work there, remained at Sullivan's right hand until 1909, assisting him with the decoration of the Schlesinger & Mayer store, and helping plan the National Farmers Bank at Owatonna.

Entrance, First National Bank, 8 West Davenport Street, Rhinelander, Wisconsin, 1910–11 (Purcell, Feick & Elmslie).

Residence of William Gray Purcell, Minneapolis, Minnesota, 1913 (Purcell & Elmslie).

Merchants National Bank of Winona, corner of Third and Lafayette Streets, Winona, Minnesota, 1911–12 (Purcell, Feick & Elmslie).

Residence of Harold C. Bradley, Madison, Wisconsin, 1914–15 (Purcell & Elmslie).

Garage and service buildings for residence of Henry Babson, Riverside, Illinois, 1915–16 (Purcell & Elmslie).

Residence of Alden B. Dow, Midland, Michigan, 1935–41.
A graduate of the University of Michigan and of the Columbia University School
of Architecture, Dow also studied under Frank Lloyd Wright at Taliesin.

ABOVE: *Ragdale, residence of Howard Van Doren Shaw, Lake Forest, Illinois,
1897 (Howard Van Doren Shaw).* BELOW: *Market Square, Lake Forest, Illinois,
1913 (Howard Van Doren Shaw). The most distinguished Chicago eclectic—
that is, the most distinguished Chicago architect who referred to historical precedent in his work—was Howard Van Doren Shaw, many of whose finest achievements may be seen in Lake Forest. The Market Square, an unusually graceful
shopping center, was commissioned by a group of businessmen headed by Cyrus
Hall McCormick II.*

ABOVE: *Residence of T. E. Donnelley, Lake Forest, Illinois, 1911 (Howard Van Doren Shaw)*. BELOW: *Residence of Prentiss Coonley, Lake Forest, Illinois, 1908 (Howard Van Doren Shaw). T. E. Donnelley was president of the printing firm of R. R. Donnelley & Sons. Prentiss Coonley was the brother of Wright's client in Riverside.*

109

ABOVE: *Entrance, residence of E. L. Ryerson, Lake Forest, Illinois, 1913 (Howard Van Doren Shaw). *BELOW: *Side view. In 1968 the steel magnate's mansion serves the needs of Saint Bonaventure's Novitiate, Order of Friars Minor.*

Residence of Stanley Keith, Lake Forest, Illinois, 1931 (David Adler). No re-
lation of Dankmar Adler, David Adler was trained in the office of Shaw. As
Christopher Tunnard has reminded us, the architects of Lake Forest owe a debt
to David Hotchkiss, who laid out the romantic plan of the town in 1856, a decade
before Frederick Law Olmsted did similar work at Riverside.

Tribune Tower, North Michigan Avenue at Chicago River, Chicago, Illinois, 1922–25 (John Mead Howells and Raymond Hood). Eliel Saarinen placed second in the gloriously advertised competition for the Tribune Tower.

Detroit Institute of Arts, 5200 Woodward Avenue, Detroit, Michigan, 1927 (Paul-Philippe Cret et al.).

ABOVE: *Capitol, Saint Paul, Minnesota, 1896–98 (Cass Gilbert).* BELOW: *Detroit Public Library, 5201 Woodward Avenue, Detroit, Michigan, 1917–21 (Cass Gilbert).*

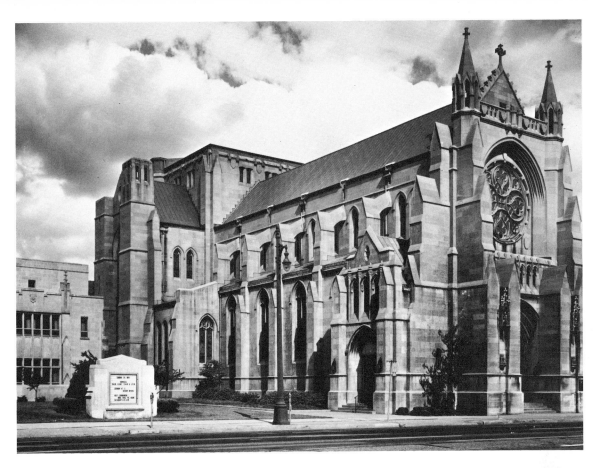

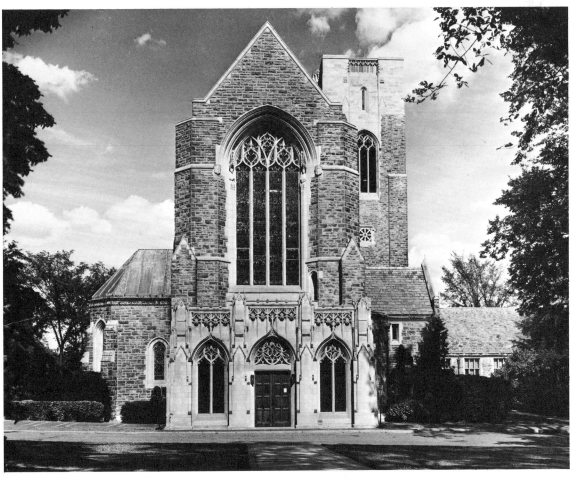

ABOVE: *Saint Paul's Cathedral, 4800 Woodward Avenue, Detroit, Michigan, 1911–19 (Ralph Adams Cram).* BELOW: *Christ Church Cranbrook, Bloomfield Hills, Michigan, 1924 (Bertram G. Goodhue Associates). Saint Paul's lacks the tower for which Cram pleaded. Christ Church Cranbrook was to have been designed by Goodhue; on his death it was completed by his office.*

Howard Hall, Principia College, Elsah, Illinois, 1935 (Bernard R. Maybeck).

Anderson Hall, Principia College, Elsah, Illinois, 1935 (Bernard R. Maybeck).
Whether Maybeck was a complete eclectic may be doubted. The inventiveness
of his Christian Science Church in Berkeley, California, has enchanted many a
modern architect in the 1960s.

ABOVE: *Villa Turicum, residence of Mr. and Mrs. Harold Fowler McCormick, Lake Forest, Illinois, 1908 (Charles A. Platt).* BELOW: *Garden Temple for Villa Turicum. Frank Lloyd Wright had hoped to win this commission, but his plans were rejected in favor of those of Platt, whose work was a charming ruin by the time these photographs were taken. Villa Turicum has since been demolished.*

117

Residence of Russell A. Alger, Jr., Grosse Pointe, Michigan, 1910 (Charles A. Platt). Built for the son of McKinley's Secretary of War, this mansion serves in 1968 as the Grosse Pointe War Memorial.

OPPOSITE ABOVE: *Entrance, Gwinn, residence of William Gwinn Mather, Cleveland, Ohio, 1907 (Charles A. Platt).* BELOW: *Gate lodge for Gwinn. William Gwinn Mather was president of the Cleveland-Cliffs Iron Co. Platt was the most talented of all the Eastern eclectics who worked in the Middle West. Gwinn may be the most distinguished house in Cleveland.*

ABOVE: *S. C. Johnson Administration Building, Racine, Wisconsin, 1936–39.*
BELOW: *Interior of the Administration Building. Virtually ignored in the conservative 1920s, Wright staged a comeback in 1936 when he built not only this temple for Johnson Wax but also Falling Water near Pittsburgh for E. J. Kaufmann.*

Research Tower for S. C. Johnson Co., Racine, Wisconsin, 1951.

Miss Johnson's wing, Wingspread, residence of Herbert F. Johnson, Jr., Racine, Wisconsin, 1937. In 1968 Wingspread serves as the headquarters of the Wingspread Foundation.

OPPOSITE: *Interior and exterior, First Unitarian Meeting House, Madison, Wisconsin, 1951.*

Apse, First Unitarian Meeting House, Madison, Wisconsin, 1951.

124

Residence of Curtis Meyer, Galesburg Village, Michigan, 1951.

Residence of William Palmer, Ann Arbor, Michigan, 1951.

Residence of Herbert Jacobs, Jr., Middleton, Wisconsin, 1950.

126

Annunciation Greek Orthodox Church, Wauwatosa, Wisconsin, 1955–61.

Residence of Carl Schultz, Saint Joseph, Michigan, 1958.

ABOVE: *Residence of Lowell Walter, Quasqueton, Iowa, 1949.* BELOW: *Boathouse for residence of Lowell Walter.*

ABOVE: *Residence of Ina Morriss Harper, Saint Joseph, Michigan, 1951.* BELOW:
Residence of Kenneth Laurent, Rockford, Illinois, 1951.

Residence of Douglas Grant, Cedar Rapids, Iowa, 1951.

OPPOSITE: *Interior and exterior, residence of Harry Neils, Minneapolis, Minnesota, 1952.*

Detail of exterior, residence of Harry Neils, Minneapolis, Minnesota, 1952.

Front and rear, residence of H. T. Mossberg, South Bend, Indiana, 1952.

Interior, residence of H. T. Mossberg, South Bend, Indiana, 1952.

OPPOSITE ABOVE: *Residence of Mrs. W. C. Alpaugh, Northport, Michigan, 1948–49.* BELOW: *Residence of Melvyn Maxwell Smith, Bloomfield Hills, Michigan, 1951. The addition to the left in the Alpaugh house is the work of Glen T. Arat & Associates.*

134

136   ABOVE: *Residence of Carroll Alsop, Oskaloosa, Iowa, 1951.* BELOW: *Residence of Charles F. Glore, Lake Forest, Illinois, 1955.*

Exterior and interior, residence of Dr. A. T. Miller, Charles City, Iowa, 1952.

Residence of Dr. Richard M. Davis, Marion, Indiana, 1954.

OPPOSITE: *Exterior and interior, residence of Bernard Schwarz, Two Rivers, Wisconsin, 1939.*

Residence of Richard Smith, Jefferson, Wisconsin, 1951.

General Motors Building, West Grand Boulevard at Cass, Detroit, Michigan, 1920.

"When I began," Kahn claimed, "the real architects would design only museums, cathedrals, capitols, monuments. The office boy was considered good enough for factories. I'm still that office boy designing factories. I have no dignity to be impaired." But Kahn was more than a factory designer. Detroit's greatest monument may be the General Motors Building, in which he followed the classical precedent of D. H. Burnham.

William L. Clements Library, Ann Arbor, Michigan, 1923. This was Kahn's favorite of all his buildings.

General Library, University of Michigan, Ann Arbor, Michigan, 1918.

Dodge Half-Ton Truck Plant, Warren, Michigan, 1938. Since this photograph was taken, considerable alterations have been made.

OPPOSITE ABOVE: *Residence of Edsel B. Ford, Grosse Pointe, Michigan, 1929.* BELOW: *Entrance drive, residence of Edsel B. Ford. The landscaping of the Ford estate was the work of Jens Jensen.*

Kingswood School for Girls, Bloomfield Hills, Michigan, 1929.

OPPOSITE ABOVE: *Colonnade, Cranbrook Academy, Bloomfield Hills, Michigan, 1940.* BELOW: *Orpheus Fountain, Cranbrook Academy, 1936 (Carl Milles).*

Detail, courtyard, Kingswood School for Girls, Bloomfield Hills, Michigan, 1929.

OPPOSITE ABOVE: *Dining room, Kingswood School for Girls, Bloomfield Hills, Michigan, 1929.* BELOW: *Front hall, Kingswood School.*

Crow Island School, Winnetka, Illinois, 1939–40. Here the Saarinens collaborated with Perkins, Wheeler & Will.

OPPOSITE ABOVE: *Tabernacle Church of Christ, Columbus, Indiana, 1940–42.* BELOW: *Interior.*

Two views of Concordia College, Fort Wayne, Indiana, 1954–58.

Jefferson Westward Expansion Memorial, Saint Louis, Missouri, 1948. In the background may be seen the Eads Bridge.

Staircase, Styling Building, General Motors Technical Center, Warren, Michigan, 1948–56.

OPPOSITE ABOVE: *Styling Building, General Motors Technical Center, Warren, Michigan 1948–56.* BELOW: *Engineering Building, General Motors Technical Center, Warren, Michigan, 1948–56. On this commission Saarinen was associated with Smith, Hinchman & Grylls.*

International Business Machines Office Buildings, Rochester, Minnesota, 1956.

OPPOSITE: *Two views, John Deere & Co., Headquarters, Moline, Illinois, 1964.*

Close-up, John Deere & Co. Headquarters, Moline, Illinois, 1964.

Crown Hall, Illinois Institute of Technology, Chicago, Illinois, 1956.

Carman Hall, Illinois Institute of Technology, Chicago, Illinois, 1954.

160

ABOVE: *Saint Savior's Chapel, Illinois Institute of Technology, Chicago, Illinois, 1952.* BELOW: *Memorial Hall, Illinois Institute of Technology, Chicago, Illinois, 1946.*

161

ABOVE: *Home Federal Building, Des Moines, Iowa, 1962.* BELOW: *School of Social Service Administration Building, 969 East 6oth Street, Chicago, Illinois, 1964.*

Lake View–Fullerton Apartments, Chicago, Illinois, 1963.

Commonwealth Promenade Apartments, Diversey Avenue and Sheridan Road,
Chicago, Illinois, 1957.

High-rise apartments, Lafayette Park, Detroit, Michigan, 1961.

Town houses, Lafayette Park, Detroit, Michigan, 1961.

860–880 Lake Shore Drive, Chicago, Illinois, 1952.

167

Federal Center, Dearborn from Adams to Jackson, Chicago, Illinois, 1964–67. Here Miës was the associate of Schmidt, Garden & Erikson, C. F. Murphy Associates, and A. Epstein and Sons.

Hedrich Blessing

Residence of Dr. Edith Farnsworth, Plano, Illinois, 1950.

ABOVE: *Inland Steel Building, 30 West Monroe Street, Chicago, Illinois, 1957.* BELOW: *Administration Building, University of Illinois at Chicago Circle, Chicago, Illinois, 1967. Walter A. Netsch was the partner in charge of this project.*

Hedrich Blessing

Close-up (with Picasso) of Civic Center, block bounded by Randolph, Washington, Dearborn and Clark, Chicago, Illinois, 1964–65. The complete credit line reads: C. F. Murphy Associates, Loebl, Schlossman & Bennett, and Skidmore, Owings & Merrill.

ABOVE: *McGregor Community Conference Center, Wayne State University, Detroit, Michigan, 1958.* BELOW: *Conservatory of Music, Oberlin College, Oberlin, Ohio, 1964.*

ABOVE: *Saint John's Abbey Church, Collegeville, Minnesota, 1962.* BELOW: *Church of Saint Francis de Sales, Muskegon, Michigan, 1967. Herbert Beckhard was Breuer's associate on the latter commission.*

173

BERTRAND GOLDBERG

ABOVE: *Marina Apartments, north bank of Chicago River, between State and Dearborn Streets, Chicago, Illinois, 1964 (Bertrand Goldberg Associates).* BELOW: *Tyrone Guthrie Theater, Minneapolis, Minnesota, 1963 (Ralph Rapson).*

RALPH RAPSON

174

ABOVE: *Housing for Hyde Park redevelopment, Chicago, Illinois, 1958.* BELOW: *Stanley R. Pierce Hall, University of Chicago, Chicago, Illinois, 1959–60. Weese was associated with I. M. Pei and Loewenberg & Loewenberg in the Hyde Park redevelopment.*

Leco Photo Service and R. Buckminster Fuller

Climatron, Botanical Gardens, Saint Louis, Missouri, 1960.

Leco Photo Service and R. Buckminster Fuller

Leco Photo Service and R. Buckminster Fuller

Interior and exterior, residence of R. Buckminster Fuller, Carbondale, Illinois, 1960. Since 1959 this most ingenious engineer has been teaching at Southern Illinois University.

Residence of John B. Swainson and Patrick Whitehead, Manistee, Michigan, 1966.

OPPOSITE ABOVE: *Student Center, Olivet College, Olivet, Michigan, 1962.* BELOW: *Entrance, Lake Michigan Hall, Grand Valley State College, Allenville, Michigan, 1967.*

BIBLIOGRAPHY

The complete file of *The Prairie School Review*, 1964–   , is an absolute necessity. This astonishing magazine, dedicated to the delightful proposition that everyone should be interested in the work of Frank Lloyd Wright and his contemporaries, is edited by W. R. Hasbrouck, 117 Fir Street, Park Forest, Illinois.

Andrews, Wayne, *Architecture, Ambition and Americans*, New York, 1955.

——, *Architecture in America*, New York, 1960.

——, *Architecture in Michigan*, Detroit, 1967.

——, *Battle for Chicago*, New York, 1946.

Barford, George, and Stanley G. Wold, eds., *Architecture in Illinois*, Springfield, 1964.

Birrell, James, *Walter Burley Griffin*, St. Lucia (Queensland, Australia), 1964.

Bragdon, Claude, "Harvey Ellis," *Architectural Review*, December, 1908.

Burnham Library of Architecture, *Buildings by Frank Lloyd Wright in Seven Middle Western States*, Chicago, 1963.

Christison, Muriel B., "How Buffington Staked His Claim," *Art Bulletin*, March, 1944.

Christ-Janer, Albert, *Eliel Saarinen*, Chicago, 1948.

Cleveland Chapter, American Institute of Architects, *A Guide to Cleveland Architecture*, New York, 1958.

Condit, Carl W., *The Chicago School of Architecture*, Chicago, 1964.

——, *The Rise of the Skyscraper*, Chicago, 1952.

Connelly, Willard, *Louis Sullivan as He Lived*, New York, 1960.

Cooper, Mabel Ruth, *Nineteenth Century Homes of Marshall, Michigan*, unpublished doctoral dissertation, Tallahassee, 1963.

Drexler, Arthur, *Ludwig Miës van der Rohe*, New York, 1962.

Eaton, Leonard K., *Landscape Artist in America: The Life and Work of Jens Jensen*, Chicago, 1965.

Egbert, Donald D., "In Search of John Edelman, Architect and Anarchist," *Journal of the American Institute of Architects*, February, 1966.

Farr, Finis, *Frank Lloyd Wright*, New York, 1961.

Ferry, W. Hawkins, "The Gothic and Tuscan Revivals in Detroit: 1828–1875," *Art Quarterly*, Summer, 1946.

——, "The Mansions of Grosse Pointe," *Monthly Bulletin of the Michigan Society of Architects*, March, 1956.

——, "Representative Detroit Buildings: A Cross Section of Architecture 1832–1943," *Bulletin of the Detroit Institute of Arts*, March, 1943.

Flanders, Robert B., *Nauvoo: Kingdom on the Mississippi*, Chicago, 1965.

Frary, I. T., *Early Homes of Ohio*, Richmond, 1936.

Fuller, R. Buckminster, *Ideas and Integrities: A Spontaneous Autobiographical Disclosure*, Englewood Cliffs, 1963.

Gebhard, David, ed., *The Work of Purcell & Elmslie*, Prairie School Press, 1965 (a reprint of *Western Architect* for January, 1913, January, 1915, and July, 1915).

Hitchcock, Henry-Russell, *The Architecture of H. H. Richardson and His Times*, New York, 1936.

——, *In the Nature of Materials 1887–1941: The Buildings of Frank Lloyd Wright*, New York, 1943.

Hoffmann, Donald, ed., *The Meanings of Architecture: Buildings and Writings by John Wellborn Root*, New York, 1967.

Jacobus, John M., *Philip Johnson*, New York, 1962.

Johannesen, Eric, "Simeon Porter: Ohio Architect," *Ohio History*, Summer, 1956.

Johnson, Philip C., *Miës van der Rohe*, New York, 1947.

Jordy, William H., and Ralph Coe, eds., *American Architecture and Other Writings by Montgomery Schuyler*, 2 vols., Cambridge, 1961.

Kaufmann, Edgar, Jr., *Louis Sullivan and the Architecture of Free Enterprise*, Chicago, 1956.

Kaufmann, Edgar, Jr., and Ben Raeburn, eds., *Frank Lloyd Wright: Writings and Buildings*, Cleveland, 1960.

Kennedy, Roger G., "Houses of the St. Croix Valley," *Minnesota History*, December, 1963.

——, "The Long Shadow of Harvey Ellis," *Minnesota History*, Fall, 1966.

——, *Minnesota Houses*, St. Paul, 1967.

Koeper, H. F., *Historic Saint Paul Buildings*, St. Paul, 1964.

"Making a Monument Work," *Architectural Forum*, July, 1958 (on the restoration of the Sullivan bank at Owatonna).

Manson, Grant C., *Frank Lloyd Wright to 1910*, New York, 1958.

McHale, John, *R. Buckminster Fuller*, New York, 1962.

McKee, Harley J., "Glimpses of Architecture—Michigan," *Michigan History*, March, 1966.

Monroe, Harriet, *John Wellborn Root*, Boston, 1896 (reissued 1966 by the Prairie School Press, Park Forest, Ill.).

Moore, Charles H., *Daniel H. Burnham*, 2 vols., Boston, 1921.

Morrison, Hugh S., "Buffington and the Invention of the Skyscraper," *Art Bulletin*, March, 1944.

——, *Louis Sullivan*, New York, 1935.

Nelson, George, *The Industrial Architecture of Albert Kahn*, New York, 1939.

Newcomb, Rexford G., *Architecture of the Old Northwest Territory*, Chicago, 1950.

Oak Park Public Library, *A Guide to the Architecture of Frank Lloyd Wright in Oak Park and River Forest, Illinois*, Oak Park, 1966.

Ohio Historical Society, *Ohio Historic Landmarks*, Columbus, 1967.

——, *Zoar: An Experiment in Communalism*, Columbus, 1966.

Peat, Wilbur D., *Indiana Houses of the Nineteenth Century*, Indianapolis, 1962.

Peisch, Mark L., *The Chicago School of Architecture: Early Followers of Sullivan and Wright*, New York, 1964.

Pickens, Buford L., "Treasure Hunting at Detroit," *Architectural Review*, December, 1944.

Rudd, J. William, *et al.*, eds., *Historic American Buildings Survey: Chicago and Nearby Areas*, Chicago, 1956.

Saarinen, Aline B., ed., *Eero Saarinen on His Work*, New Haven, 1962.

Scully, Vincent, Jr., *Frank Lloyd Wright*, New York, 1960.

Siegel, Arthur, ed., *Chicago's Famous Buildings*, Chicago, 1965.

Smith, Norris Kelly, *Frank Lloyd Wright: A Study in Architectural Content*, New York, 1966.

Sullivan, Louis H., *The Autobiography of an Idea*, New York, 1924.

——, *Democracy*, Detroit, 1961.

——, *Kindergarten Chats*, New York, 1947.

——, *A System of Architectural Ornament*, New York, 1924.

Swales, Francis S., "Harvey Ellis," *Pencil Points*, July, 1924.

Tallmadge, Thomas E., *Architecture in Old Chicago*, Chicago, 1941.

Temko, Allan, *Eero Saarinen*, New York, 1962.

Torbert, Donald R., *A Century of Art and Architecture in Minnesota*, Minneapolis, 1958.

——, *A Century of Minnesota Architecture*, Minneapolis, 1958.

Tselos, Dimitri, "The Enigma of Buffington's Skyscraper," *Art Bulletin*, March, 1944.

——, "Exotic Influences in the Work of Frank Lloyd Wright," *Magazine of Art*, April, 1953.

Tunnard, Christopher, *The City of Man*, New York, 1953.

"Tyrone Guthrie Theater," *Design Quarterly 58*, Minneapolis, 1963.

Upjohn, Everard M., "Buffington and the Skyscraper," *Art Bulletin*, March, 1944.

Webster, J. Carson, *Architecture of Chicago and Vicinity*, Society of Architectural Historians, Media, Pa., 1965.

Wright, Frank Lloyd, *An Autobiography*, New York, 1932.

——, *Drawings for a Living Architecture*, New York, 1959.

——, *Frank Lloyd Wright on Architecture*, edited by Frederick Gutheim, New York, 1941.

——, *The Future of Architecture*, New York, 1953.

——, *Genius and the Mobocracy*, New York, 1949.

——, *The Living City*, New York, 1958.

——, *The Natural House*, New York, 1954.

——, *A New House on Bear Run, Pennsylvania, by Frank Lloyd Wright*, New York, 1938.

——, *The Story of the Tower*, New York, 1956.

——, *Taliesin Drawings*, New York, 1952.

——, *A Testament*, New York, 1931.

Wright, John Lloyd, *My Father Who Is on Earth*, New York, 1946.

INDEX (ARCHITECTS IN ITALICS)

Adler, Dankmar, 111; see also *Adler & Sullivan*
Adler, Dankmar & Co., 48
Adler & Sullivan, 45–53
Adler, David, 111
Administration Building, University of Illinois at Chicago Circle, Chicago, Ill., 170
Administration Building, World's Fair of 1893, 61
Agricultural Building, World's Fair of 1893, 62
Alger, Russell A., Jr., res., Grosse Pointe, Mich., 118
Allen, Benjamin Franklin, res., Des Moines, Ia., 15
Allenville, Mich., 178
Alpaugh, Mrs. W. C., res., Northport, Mich., 135
Alsop, Carroll, res., Oskaloosa, Ia., 136
Amberg, J. H., res., Grand Rapids, Mich., 89
Anderson Hall, Principia College, Elsah, Ill., 116
Ann Arbor, Mich., 13, 126, 142–143
Anna, Ill., 92
Annunciation Greek Orthodox Church, Wauwatosa, Wis., 127
Arat, Glenn T., & Associates, 135
Art Building, World's Fair of 1893, 63
Atwood, Charles B., 43, 63
Auditorium, Chicago, Ill., 45–47
Aurora, Ind., 9
Austin, Henry, 8
Avery-Downer house, Granville, O., 14

Babson, Henry, res., Riverside, Ill., 59; garage, Riverside, Ill., 106
Balch, Emil, res., Chicago, Ill., 75
Bäumeler, Joseph, 6
Beachy, P. A., res., Oak Park, Ill., 73
Beckhard, Herbert, 173
Beman, Solon Spencer, 34–35
Bishop Hill, Ill., 5
Bloomfield Hills, Mich., 115, 135, 146–149
Blossom, George, res., Chicago, Ill., 65
Borden, William, res., Chicago, Ill., 22
Borden Block, Chicago, Ill., 48
Boyington, W. W., 15–16
Bradley, B. Harley, res., Kankakee, Ill., 76
Bradley, Harold C., res., Madison, Wis., 105

Bradley, Josephine Crane, res., Madison, Wis., 59
Breuer, Marcel, 173
Brookfield, Ill., 98
Brookfield Kindergarten, Brookfield, Ill., 98
Buffington, L. S., 20, 31
Burnham, D. H., 94, 96, 141; see also *Burnham & Root*
Burnham, D. H., & Co., 44
Burnham & Root, 40–43, 85
Byrne, Barry, 93

Capitol, St. Paul, Minn., 114
Carbondale, Ill., 177
Carman Hall, Illinois Institute of Technology, Chicago, Ill., 160
Carson, Pirie Scott & Co., Chicago, Ill., 54–55, 101
Castellane, Boni de, 29
Cedar Rapids, Ia., 130
Chapin & Gore Building, Chicago, Ill., 86
Charles City, Ia., 137
Charnley, James, res., Chicago, Ill., 67
Cheney, E. H., res., Oak Park, Ill., 80
Cheney, Mamah Borthwick, 89
Chicago, Ill., 16, 19, 21–25, 27, 29, 36–50, 52–55, 60–65, 67, 72, 75, 85–88, 99, 112, 159–164, 167–171, 174–175
Chicago, University of, Stanley R. Pierce Hall, 175
Chicago Historical Society Building, Chicago, Ill., 27
Chicago Plan, 44
Chicago Water Tower, Chicago, Ill., 15
Christ Church Cranbrook, Bloomfield Hills, Mich., 115
Civic Center, Chicago, Ill., 171
Clarke, J. F., res., Fairfield, Ia., 93
Clements, William L., Library, Ann Arbor, Mich., 142
Cleveland, O., 117
Climatron, St. Louis, Mo., 176
Cobb, Henry Ives, 27–29, 63
Collegeville, Minn., 173
Columbus, Ind., 150
Columbus, Wis., 56
Commonwealth-Promenade Apts., Chicago, Ill., 164
Communal housing, Bishop Hill, Ill., 5
Comstock, Hurd, house for, Evanston, Ill., 91
Concordia College, Ft. Wayne, Ind., 152

Condit, Carl W., 37
Coonley, Avery, res., Riverside, Ill., 78; playhouse for res., Riverside, Ill., 79
Coonley, Mrs. Avery, 98–99
Coonley, Prentiss, res., Lake Forest, Ill., 109
Cram, Ralph Adams, 115
Cranbrook Academy, Bloomfield Hills, Mich., 146
Cret, Paul-Philippe, 113
Crow Island School, Winnetka, Ill., 151
Crown Hall, Illinois Institute of Technology, Chicago, Ill., 159
Cudell & Blumenthal, 19

Dana, Susan Lawrence, res., Springfield, Ill., 80
Davis, Dr. Richard M., res., Marion, Ind., 139
Decatur, Ill., 89
Deere, John, & Co., Headquarters, Moline, Ill., 157–158
Des Moines, Ia., 15, 162
Detroit, Mich., 26, 113–115, 141, 165–166, 172
Detroit Institute of Arts, Detroit, Mich., 113
Detroit Public Library, Detroit, Mich., 114
Dodge Half-Ton Truck Plant, Warren, Mich., 144
Donnelley, T. E., res., Lake Forest, Ill., 109
Dow, Alden B., 107
Drummond, William, 98–100; see also *Guenzel & Drummond*

Eads, James Buchanan, 20
Eads Bridge, St. Louis, Mo., 20, 153
Eckel & Mann, 31
860–880 Lake Shore Drive, Chicago, Ill., 167
Ellis, Harvey, 31–33
Elms, The, Hudson, O., 8
Elmslie, George Grant, 55, 57, 101–106; see also *Purcell & Elmslie* and *Purcell, Feick & Elmslie*
Elsah, Ill., 116
Epstein, A., & Sons, 168
Evanston, Ill., 91, 94
Eyre, Wilson, Jr., 26

Fairbank, N. K., res., Lake Geneva, Wis., 18
Fairfield, Ia., 93

Farmers & Merchants Union Bank, Columbus, Wis., 56
Farnsworth, Dr. Edith, res., Plano, Ill., 169
Federal Center, Chicago, Ill., 168
Feick, George, 101; see also *Purcell, Feick & Elmslie*
Field, Marshall, res., Chicago, Ill., 22, 30; wholesale store, Chicago, Ill., 23
First Congregational Church of Austin, Chicago, Ill., 99
First National Bank, Rhinelander, Wis., 102
First Unitarian Meeting House, Madison, Wis., 123–124
Fisheries Building, World's Fair of 1893, 63
Ford, Edsel B., res., Grosse Pointe, Mich., 145
Fort Wayne, Ind., 152
Freer, Charles Lang, res., Detroit, Mich., 26
Fricke, W. G., res., Oak Park, Ill., 73
Frost, Charles S., 28
Fuller, R. Buckminster, 176–177

Gaff, Thomas, res., Aurora, Ind., 9
Galena, Ill., 12
Galesburg Village, Mich., 125
Garden, Hugh M. G., 86–88; see also *Schmidt, Garden & Martin*
Garrick Theatre Building, Chicago, Ill., 48
General Library, University of Michigan, Ann Arbor, Mich., 143
General Motors Building, Detroit, Mich., 141; Technical Center, Warren, Mich., 154–155
Getty, Carrie Eliza, tomb of, Chicago, Ill., 52
Gilbert, Cass, 114
Gilmore, E. A., res., Madison, Wis., 82
Glessner, John J., res., Chicago, Ill., 24–25
Glore, Charles F., res., Lake Forest, Ill., 136
Goldberg, Bertrand, Associates, 174
Goldmark, Karl, 19
Goodhue, B. G., Associates, 115
Grand Rapids, Mich., 82, 89
Grand Valley State College, Allenville, Mich., 178
Grant, Douglas, res., Cedar Rapids, Ia., 130
Granville, O., 14
Griffin, Walter Burley, 89–92
Grinnell, Ia., 56

Grosse Ile, Mich., 10
Grosse Pointe, Mich., 118, 145
Guenzel, Louis, 98–100
Guenzel & Drummond, 98–100
Guthrie, Tyrone, Theatre, Minneapolis, Minn., 174

Hanna, Marcus Alonzo, 35
Hardy, Thomas P., res., Racine, Wis., 74
Harper, Ina Morriss, res., St. Joseph, Mich., 129
Harris, Harwell Hamilton, 58
Hays, Dr. Andrew L., res., Marshall, Mich., 7
Heller, Isidor, res., Chicago, Ill., 65
Herrick, Robert, res., Chicago, Ill., 88
Hickox, Warren, res., Kankakee, Ill., 77
Highland Park, Ill., 68
Hill, James J., res., St. Paul, Minn., 30
Hillforest, Aurora, Ind., 9
Holabird & Roche, 38–39
Holst, Hermann von, 89
Home Federal Building, Des Moines, Ia., 162
Home Insurance Building, Chicago, Ill., 36
Hood, Raymond, 112
Hotchkiss, David, 111
Hotel Florence, Pullman, Ill., 35
Howard, John Galen, 101
Howard Hall, Principia College, Elsah, Ill., 116
Howells, John Mead, 112
Hudson, O., 8
Hudson, Wis., 11–12
Hunt, Richard Morris, 22, 61
Hyde Park Redevelopment, Chicago, Ill., 175

Illinois, University of, Chicago Circle, Chicago, Ill., 170
Illinois Institute of Technology, Chicago, Ill., 159–161
Inland Steel Building, Chicago, Ill., 170
International Business Machine Office Buildings, Rochester, Minn., 156

Jacobs, Herbert, res., Middleton, Wis., 126
James, Henry, 15
Jefferson, Wis., 140

Jefferson Westward Expansion Memorial, St. Louis, Mo., 153
Jenney, William Le Baron, 36–37
Jensen, Jens, 145
Johnson, Herbert F., Jr., res., Racine, Wis., 122
Johnson, Philip C., 4
Johnson, S. C., Administration Building, Racine, Wis., 120; Research Tower, Racine, Wis., 121
Jones, J. Russell, res., Galena, Ill., 12

Kahn, Albert, 141–145
Kankakee, Ill., 76–77
Kaufmann, Edgar, Jr., 120
Keith, Stanley, res., Lake Forest, Ill., 111
Kenilworth, Ill., 94–95
Kenilworth Club, Kenilworth, Ill., 94
Kennedy, Roger G., 31
Kingswood School, Bloomfield Hills, Mich., 147–149
Kirtland, O., 2
Krause Music Store and residence, Chicago, Ill., 60

Lafayette Park, Detroit, Mich., 165–166
Lake Forest, Ill., 27, 108–111, 117, 136
Lake Geneva, Wis., 18
Lake View–Fullerton Apts., Chicago, Ill., 163
Latrobe, Benjamin Henry, 7
Laurent, Kenneth, res., Rockford, Ill., 129
Leiter Building I, Chicago, Ill., 37
Lewis, Charles H., res., Hudson, Wis., 12
Lipchitz, Jacques, 4
Little, Francis W., res., Peoria, Ill., 77
Lloyd, Gordon W., 10
Loebl, Schlossman & Bennett, 171
Loewenberg & Loewenberg, 175

MacVeagh, Franklin, res., Chicago, Ill., 24
Madison, Wis., 59, 82, 105, 123–124
Madlener, Albert F., res., Chicago, Ill., 87
Maher, George W., 94–97
Mahony, Marion, 89
Manistee, Mich., 179
Manufactures Building, World's Fair of 1893, 62
Marina Apts., Chicago, Ill., 174
Marion, Ind., 139

Market Square, Lake Forest, Ill., 108
Marshall, Mich., 7–8
Martin, Edgar, 86; see also *Schmidt, Garden & Martin*
Martin, W. E., res., Oak Park, Ill., 75
Mason City, Ia., 90–91
Masonic Temple, Chicago, Ill., 42
Mather, W. G., res., Cleveland, O., 119
May, Meyer, res., Grand Rapids, Mich., 82
Maybeck, Bernard R., 116
McAllister, James W., res., St. Joseph, Mo., 33
McCormick, Cyrus Hall, res., Chicago, Ill., 19, 21
McCormick, Cyrus Hall II, 19, 108
McCormick, Mr. and Mrs. Harold Fowler, res., Lake Forest, Ill., 117
McGregor Community Conference Center, Wayne State University, Detroit, Mich., 172
McKim, Mead & White, 62
Meathe, Kessler Associates, 178–179
Melson, J. G., res., Mason City, Ia., 90
Memorial Hall, Illinois Institute of Technology, Chicago, Ill., 161
Menomonie, Wis., 31–32
Merchants Bank of Winona, Winona, Minn., 104
Merchants National Bank, Grinnell, Ia., 56
Meyer, Curtis, res., Galesburg Village, Mich., 125
Middleton, Wis., 126
Midland, Mich., 107
Midway Gardens, Chicago, Ill., 81
Miës van der Rohe, Ludwig, 159–169
Milan, O., 10
Miller, Dr. A. T., res., Charles City, Ia., 137
Milles, Carl, 146
Milwaukee, Wis., 19
Minneapolis, Minn., 20, 103, 131–132, 174
Mitchell, Alexander, res., Milwaukee, Wis., 19
Mitchell-Turner house, Milan, O., 10
Moffat, John S., res., Hudson, Wis., 11
Moline, Ill., 157–158
Monadnock Building, Chicago, Ill., 40
Monroe Building, Chicago, Ill., 39
Morgan, Benjamin, 14
Mormon Temple, Kirtland, O., 2
Mormon Temple, Nauvoo, Ill., 1
Mossberg, H. T., res., South Bend, Ind., 133–134

Motter, Joshua, res., St. Joseph, Mo., 32
Mueller, Robert, res., Decatur, Ill., 89
Murphy, C. F., Associates, 168, 171
Museum of Science and Industry, Chicago, Ill., 63
Muskegon, Mich., 173

National Farmers Bank, Owatonna, Minn., 57–58, 101
Nauvoo, Ill., 1
Neils, Harry, res., Minneapolis, Minn., 131–132
Netsch, Walter A., 170
New Harmony, Ind., 4
Newberry Library, Chicago, Ill., 27
Northport, Mich., 135
Number One House, Zoar, O., 6

Oak Park, Ill., 69–70, 73, 75, 80, 97
Oberlin, O., 172
Oberlin College, Oberlin, O., 172
Old State Bank, Shawneetown, Ill., 13
Olivet, Mich., 178
Olivet College Student Center, Olivet, Mich., 178
Olmsted, Frederick Law, 111
Olson, Olaf, 5
Orpheus Fountain, Cranbrook, Bloomfield Hills, Mich., 146
Oskaloosa, Ia., 136
Owatonna, Minn., 57–58
Owen, David Dale, 3
Owen, Robert Dale, 3

Page, Harry, res., Mason City, Ia., 91
Palmer, Potter, res., Chicago, Ill., 29
Palmer, William, res., Ann Arbor, Mich., 126
Palmer House, Chicago, Ill., 21
Patten, James A., 94
Peabody & Stearns, 30
Pei, I. M., 175
People's Savings & Loan Association Building, Sidney, O., 54
Peoria, Ill., 77
Perkins, Dwight H., 85
Perkins, Wheeler & Will, 151
Picasso, Pablo, 171
Pierce Hall, University of Chicago, Chicago, Ill., 175
Pillsbury "A" Mill, Minneapolis, Minn., 20
Plano, Ill., 169
Platt, Abner, res., Marshall, Mich., 8
Platt, Charles A., 117–119

Pond, I. K., 34–35
Porter, Simeon (?), 8
Post, George B., 62
Presbyterian Church, Lake Forest, Ill., 27
Principia College, Elsah, Ill., 116
Pullman, George Mortimer, 35
Pullman, Ill., 34–35
Pullman housing, Pullman, Ill., 34; works, Pullman, Ill., 34
Purcell, William G., 103; see also *Purcell & Elmslie* and *Purcell, Feick & Elmslie*
Purcell & Elmslie, 101–106
Purcell, Feick & Elmslie, 102, 104

Quasqueton, Ia., 128

Racine, Wis., 74, 120–122
Railway Exchange Building, Chicago, Ill., 44
Rapson, Ralph, 174
Reliance Building, Chicago, Ill., 43
Renwick, James, Jr., 3
Rhinelander, Wis., 102
Richardson, H. H., 23–25
River Forest, Ill., 66, 71, 100
Riverside, Ill., 59, 71, 78–79, 99–106, 111
Roberts, Isabel, res., River Forest, Ill., 71
Robie, Frederick C., res., Chicago, Ill., 72
Rochester, Minn., 156
Rockford, Ill., 129
Roofless Church, New Harmony, Ind., 4
Rookery Building, Chicago, Ill., 42, 67
Root, John Wellborn, 40–44, 85; see also *Burnham & Root*
Ryerson, E. L., res., Lake Forest, Ill., 110
Ryerson, Martin, tomb of, Chicago, Ill., 50

Saarinen, Eero, 150–158
Saarinen, Eliel, 112, 146–151
St. Francis de Sales Church, Muskegon, Mich., 173
St. James Church, Grosse Ile, Mich., 10
St. John's Abbey Church, Collegeville, Minn., 173
St. Joseph, Mich., 127, 129
St. Joseph, Mo., 32–33
St. Louis, Mo., 20, 33, 50–51, 153, 176

St. Paul, Minn., 30, 114
St. Paul's Cathedral, Detroit, Mich., 115
St. Savior's Chapel, Illinois Institute of Technology, Chicago, Ill., 161
Schiller Building, Chicago, Ill., 48–49
Schlesinger & Mayer store, Chicago, Ill., 54–55, 101
Schmidt, Garden & Eriksen, 168
Schmidt, Garden & Martin, 86–87
Schmidt, Richard E., 86–87
School of Social Service Administration, Chicago, Ill., 162
Schultz, Carl, res., St. Joseph, Mich., 127
Schurz, Carl, School, Chicago, Ill., 85
Schwarz, Bernard, res., Two Rivers, Wis., 138
Sears, Joseph, School, Kenilworth, Ill., 94
Shaw, Howard Van Doren, 108–111
Shawneetown, Ill., 13
Sidney, O., 54
Silsbee, J. L., 94
Sioux City, Ia., 101
Skidmore, Owings & Merrill, 170–171
Smith, Hinchman & Grylls, 154
Smith, Joseph, 1
Smith, Melvyn Maxwell, res., Bloomfield Hills, Mich., 135
Smith, Richard, res., Jefferson, Wis., 140
South Bend, Ind., 28, 133–134
Spring Green, Wis., 83–84
Springfield, Ill., 80
Steele, William L., 101
Steeple Building, Bishop Hill, Ill., 5
Stevens, J. Walter, 31
Stevenson, Adlai E., 22
Stinson Library, Anna, Ill., 92
Stock Exchange Building, Chicago, Ill., 53
Studebaker, Clement, res., South Bend, Ind., 28

Student Center, Olivet College, Olivet, Mich., 178
Sullivan, Louis H., 23, 45–60, 64, 101
Swainson, John B., res., Manistee, Mich., 179

Tabernacle Church of Christ, Columbus, Ind., 150
Tacoma Building, Chicago, Ill., 38
Tainter, Mabel, Memorial, Menomonie, Wis., 31–32
Taliesin East, Spring Green, Wis., 83–84
Taylor, J. Hall, res., Oak Park, Ill., 97
Thorncroft, Riverside, Ill., 99
Tolan, Thomas J., 17
Tomek, F. F., res., Riverside, Ill., 71
Transportation Building, World's Fair of 1893, 64
Treat & Foltz, 18
Tribune Tower, Chicago, Ill., 112
Tselos, Dimitri, 20, 64
Tunnard, Christopher, 111
Two Rivers, Wis., 138

Unitarian Universalist Church, Oak Park, Ill., 69–70
Unity Temple, Oak Park, Ill., 69–70
University Club, Chicago, Ill., 39

Van Osdel, John Mills, 21
Van Wert, O., 17
Van Wert County Courthouse, Van Wert, O., 17

Wainwright, Charlotte Dickson, tomb of, St. Louis, Mo., 50
Wainwright Building, St. Louis, Mo., 51

Walter, Lowell, res., Quasqueton, Ia., 128
Ward, Montgomery, Warehouse, Chicago, Ill., 87
Warren, Mich., 144, 154–155
Washington Terrace, St. Louis, Mo., 33
Wauwatosa, Wis., 127
Wayne State University, Detroit, Mich., 172
Weese, Harry M., & Associates, 46–47, 175
Wheeler, John M., res., Ann Arbor, Mich., 13
Whistler, James Abbott McNeill, 22, 26
Whitehead, Patrick, res., Manistee, Mich., 179
Wilde, Oscar, 116
Willitts, Ward W., res., Highland Park, Ill., 68
Wingspread, res., Herbert F. Johnson, Jr., Racine, Wis., 122
Winnetka, Ill., 151
Winona, Minn., 96, 104
Winona Savings Bank, Winona, Minn., 96
Winslow, W. H., res., River Forest, Ill., 66
Woman's Temple, Chicago, Ill., 41
Women's Club, River Forest, Ill., 100
Woodbury County Courthouse, Sioux City, Ia., 101
World's Fair of 1893, 61–64
Wright, Frank Lloyd, 42, 65–84, 89–90, 93–94, 98, 101, 107, 117, 120–140

Yamasaki, Minoru, 172

Zoar, O., 6

WAYNE ANDREWS

Born in Kenilworth, Illinois, in 1913, Mr. Andrews was educated in the Winnetka public schools, Lawrenceville School, and Harvard College. Later he received his doctorate in American history at Columbia University under the sponsorship of Allan Nevins. From 1948 to 1956 he was Curator of Manuscripts at the New-York Historical Society. From 1956 to 1963 he was an editor at Charles Scribner's Sons. Since 1964 he has been Archives of American Art Professor at Wayne State University, Detroit.

Mr. Andrews is the author of The Vanderbilt Legend (*1941*), Battle for Chicago (*1946*), Architecture, Ambition and Americans (*1955*), Architecture in America (*1960*), Germaine: A Portrait of Madame de Staël (*1963*) *and* Architecture in Michigan, (*1967*). *He is also the editor of* The Best Short Stories of Edith Wharton (*1958*), *and under the pseudonym Montagu O'Reilly is the author of* Who Has Been Tampering with These Pianos? *He has contributed to such publications as* The Architectural Review, Town and Country, House Beautiful, House and Garden, Harper's, Harper's Bazaar, The Saturday Review *and* The New York Times. *He is also a former president of the New York chapter of the Society of Architectural Historians.*